PASSION ISN'T ENOUGH:

A Practical Guide
for Nonprofit Leaders

David Rhode

Red Thread Publishing LLC. 2024
Red Falcon Press is an imprint of Red Thread Publishing.

Write to info@redthreadbooks.com if you are interested in publishing with Red Thread Publishing. Learn more about publications or foreign rights acquisitions of our catalog of books: www.redthreadbooks.com

Copyright © 2024 by David Rhode
All rights reserved.

No part of this book may be reproduced in any form or means. Any unauthorized use, sharing, reproduction or distribution of these materials by any means, electronic, mechanical or otherwise is strictly prohibited. No portion of these materials may be reproduced in any manner whatsoever, without the express written consent of the publisher and the author, except for the use of brief quotations in a book review.

Paperback ISBN: 979-8-89294-018-4
Ebook ISBN: 979-8-89294-019-1

What people are saying about
Passion Isn't Enough

◆◆━━━━━◆◆◆━━━━━◆◆

"If you're running a nonprofit enterprise, this is the manual for you. Drawing on his own nonprofit leadership and that of others, David Rhode compiles tangible, experienced advice on everything from strategic plans and stakeholder feedback to building your board, branding the enterprise, and surmounting a crisis. *Passion Isn't Enough* is the handbook for getting nonprofit things done."

– MICHAEL USEEM,
Faculty Director of the McNulty Leadership Program, Wharton School, University of Pennsylvania, and author of *The Edge: How 10 CEOs Learned to Lead*

Real, inspiring, actionable. As a young nonprofit executive, I felt confident that I could implement these lessons in my organization today! *Passion Isn't Enough* is a must read for any nonprofit leader ready to take their organization to the next level!"

– ELI MORARU,
Co-Founder and President The Community Grocer (TCG Groceries)

"David Rhode's book is an invaluable guide for leaders looking to transform their passion into real impact! He translates his years of experience into tangible advice and next steps on how to lead a nonprofit with ease, efficiency, and joy."

— Lauren Blodgett,
Founder, The Brave House

"David Rhode's guide is a breath of fresh air. It's like having a mentor by your side, offering relatable advice and breaking down complex ideas into digestible nuggets of wisdom. With real-world examples and a conversational style, you can jump into any chapter at any time—there is no need to read them in order or all at once. It's a flexible guide you can pick up whenever needed."

— Erin Salazar,
Founder and Executive Director, Local Color

"David Rhode's *Passion Isn't Enough* transcends typical nonprofit guides by offering deeply practical and insightful advice. His real-world examples and strategic frameworks make this an invaluable resource that every nonprofit leader should have on their shelf."

— Nathan Chappell,
AI inventor and co-author of the "Generosity Crisis: The Case for Radical Connection to Solve Humanity's Greatest Challenges.

DEDICATION

*This book is dedicated to
all the generous leaders
who have helped me along the way.*

TABLE OF CONTENTS

INTRODUCTION 1

CHAPTER 1: Building Your Strategic Plan 7

CHAPTER 2: Building Your Board 27

CHAPTER 3: Building Your Fundraising Strategy 45

CHAPTER 4: Building Your Partnership Portfolio 75

CHAPTER 5: Building Your Financial Controls 93

CHAPTER 6: Building Your Programs 105

CHAPTER 7: Building Your Evidence Base 117

CHAPTER 8: Building Your Brand 133

CHAPTER 9: Building Your Communications Strategy 151

CHAPTER 10: Building Your AI Capabilities 167

CHAPTER 11: Building Your Team 179

CHAPTER 12: Building Your Diverse Organization 191

CHAPTER 13: Building Your Volunteer Community 205

CHAPTER 14: Building Your Crisis Response 219

CHAPTER 15: Building Your Exit Strategy 229

CHAPTER 16: Advice For New Leaders 245

CONTRIBUTOR PROFILES 253

ACKNOWLEDGMENTS 299

ABOUT THE AUTHOR 301

THANK YOU! 303

INTRODUCTION

"Am I in over my head?"
"Which fires should I try to put out first?"
"What do I do if I can't hit my budget number?"

Do these questions sound familiar?

In 2005, I launched Pitch In for Baseball and Softball, a nonprofit organization to help kids in the United States and worldwide gain access to playing baseball and softball. We did this by sending new and gently used equipment to leagues, schools, and regions that lacked those essential resources. The 14+ years where I led and scaled this organization were some of the most rewarding, engaging, and memorable experiences of my professional life. We helped over a million kids in over 100 countries around the world. We became best known for assisting countless towns to recover from natural disasters by getting them back on the baseball and softball field after their worlds had turned upside down. Reuniting kids with their friends and giving their families and communities "a sense of normalcy" in a time of tremendous uncertainty became repeated themes we heard that described our work's real impact. The most vivid memories during my tenure at Pitch In for Baseball and Softball are from these disaster relief efforts. I can still picture the faces and hear the voices of so many grateful kids, parents, and coaches.

When I began my nonprofit leadership journey, people frequently remarked on how passionate I was as they wished me well on my mission-driven venture. I plunged ahead with a lot of confidence and a dearth of nonprofit sector experience. During the early part of my nonprofit career I got many things right but a lot of things wrong. In other cases, I just didn't know what I didn't know. One of my biggest hopes for this book is that aspiring leaders in the nonprofit sector can learn from the experience I've gained over the years, avoid some of the most significant problems I had to endure, and learn how to build on the things they already do well.

Since my time leading Pitch In for Baseball and Softball, I've been fortunate to have the opportunity to evaluate the nonprofit sector in a wide variety of ways. I founded a consultancy, dotdotorg.com, through which I've been able to mentor countless nonprofits and their executive teams through all manner of challenges. In my work as Deputy Director of PennPAC, an organization that mobilizes teams of University of Pennsylvania alumni to strengthen the nonprofit sector, I have had the chance to become acquainted with dozens and dozens of the most inspiring mission-driven agencies and see the challenges they are facing. I also have the privilege of teaching Nonprofit Branding at the University of Pennsylvania's School of Social Policy and

Practice, as well as nonprofit consulting at the Wharton School, and through this work I've been able to meet, educate, and partner with the next generation of nonprofit leaders and executives from a range of disciplines, geographies, and backgrounds.

Through all of this work, looking at the sector through all of these different lenses and perspectives, I have found that the same challenges come up over and over again. Regardless of the organization's mission, or the size of the agency, or whatever else, the same problems always seem to arise. It's for this reason that I write this book, to offer to you - one of our next great nonprofit leaders - practical and proven solutions to some of the common challenges you'll likely face on your journey.

Time and again, as both a coach and a consultant, I have been asked about issues like how to attack a strategic plan, how to develop a more engaged and effective board, and how to more successfully fundraise to increase organizational capacity. This book addresses these challenges and many more. While it can be read sequentially, it doesn't need to be. Go to where you are experiencing the most pain. Go to what interests you the most.

In this book, you'll find frameworks and tools to help develop and execute a strategic plan, think through your branding and communications needs, manage your staff and volunteers, expand your portfolio of strategic partners, help guide your board through their role in the organization's success, and more. These are tools that you can utilize right now to make a difference in your organization.

You will also hear from more than twenty highly-talented nonprofit CEOs and subject matter experts throughout this book, who all generously gave of their time to offer insights, support, and best practices for nonprofit executives. These are leaders who I know and respect, and who collectively have over 450 years of experience in the sector. Many of them have helped me along the way, and their advice and structured approaches to problem solving will help you too.

This isn't a textbook or a legal guide to running a nonprofit…there are already plenty of those out there for you to learn from. This book is about sitting in the big chair and leading an organization. It is about sharing knowledge, embracing the community of nonprofit leaders, lifting up people doing important work, and helping you further the mission of your respective organizations.

There are approximately 1.8 million nonprofit CEOs/Executive Directors in the United States alone[1]. According to the National Council of Nonprofits, a staggering 92% of these organizations have operating budgets of $1 million or less[2]. If my over twenty years of experience leading and consulting in the sector have taught me anything, it's that almost all of these leaders could benefit from some form of assistance.

I wrote this book with these nonprofit leaders in mind. I've walked in your shoes, heard the stories and secrets, experienced the frustrations, and shared in the triumphs. I have a good

---

[1] "Nonprofit Trends and Impacts 2021", Urban Institute, last modified October 26, 2021, https://www.urban.org/sites/default/files/publication/104889/nonprofit-trends-and-impacts-2021_2.pdf

[2] "Downloadable Charts and Figures", Nonprofit Impact Matters, National Council of Nonprofits, 2019, https://www.nonprofitimpactmatters.org/data/downloadable-charts/

sense of where you get stuck and some proven and practical solutions to get you unstuck. Young or inexperienced leaders don't need more passion; they need more support. This book seeks to provide it.

I hope you enjoy the journey!

CHAPTER 1:
Building Your Strategic Plan

Chapter Overview: This chapter highlights the role of strategic planning in an organization and provides an overview of the primary steps in the planning process.

How does your nonprofit make critical decisions about new opportunities, resource allocation, and matters of organizational importance? Are those decisions made within the confines of a particular conversation or board meeting, or are they part of a larger more thoughtful strategic plan?

Strategic planning is a widely discussed topic in the nonprofit sector. It's also often misunderstood or misinterpreted. So what is a strategic plan and how do you create one?

What is a Strategic Plan and Why Should You Have One?

Think of strategic planning in its simplest terms. It's creating a roadmap. And like any good roadmap, it shows you (in theory) the most efficient way to get to your desired destination. It defines success for your organization, with a focused plan on which opportunities or challenges your team may need to address to reach success as you define it. It is a tool to help align the board and staff on the top priorities with direct implications on how resources, both people and dollars, will be allocated. From the nonprofit CEO's perspective, it is also a tool that helps you say "no" to ideas and opportunities that distract or drain resources from agreed upon priorities.

Before going through the actual steps in the process, let's reflect on what the plan is trying to accomplish. Done correctly, a strategic plan will outline where you are now as an organization, where you want to go in the next three (or however many) years, what obstacles are preventing you from getting there, and what is needed to reach your desired state. It's a plan with measurable goals, strategies to achieve those goals, tactics to implement those strategies, and clarity about who is responsible for crucial steps along the way. A strategic plan shouldn't be an over twenty-page undertaking that ultimately collects dust on the shelf. Most of the critical narratives should be able to be accomplished in a few pages, potentially only one. The strategic plan should be a dynamic document that is shared widely with staff, board, stakeholders, and funders, both internally and externally.

How Far Ahead Should My Strategic Plan Look?

A strategic plan is an organization's collective best thinking. It articulates which areas the agency believes will have the most significant leverage for organizational growth and sustainability. Effectively, it is a bet on the future of the entire organization. If we channel our scarce resources, both staff and budgetary, on these three or four priorities over an extended period of time, we believe we can put the organization on a better trajectory for long-term success. Success as we define it. Getting the list of goals narrowed down to those precious few is both the beauty and inherent challenge that awaits any organization embarking on strategic planning. Having the collective discipline to narrow the list will most likely make some board members or staff uncomfortable. It also means that some things won't make the final list. Not making the final list doesn't mean an idea is inadequate or unworthy. It simply acknowledges that a lean staff and a tight budget can't take on everything and that some ideas or focus areas may have more profound and longer-term value than others.

Brooke Richie-Babbage is a former nonprofit founder turned social impact strategist and coach. Much of her work with clients encompasses strategic plan development. In fact, she describes herself as a "unapologetic strategy geek". She holds the belief that most organizations should be able to come up with a strategic plan in four months or less. Conversely, a plan that might take nine months (or longer) to develop assumes that the organization has been stagnant during that extended plan development period. In reality, over a nine-month window of time an organization's budgets, staff, board and more can all change. In fact, the world around us could change.

One thing that Brooke stresses in her work is a simple, single-page strategic plan outlining the organization's vision, goals, and focus areas. In my view, the beauty in Brooke's approach is in what she calls the development of three anchor documents: the strategic plan, the budget, and the development plan.

All too often, organizations develop their strategic plan in a vacuum. Likewise, the budget development and resource development process are tackled as independent and disconnected workstreams. In Brooke's three anchor documents approach, the strategic plan outlines the priorities, the budget outlines what the organization will need to spend to achieve its goals, and the resource development plan identifies how the organization is going to attract the requisite resources to take on its myriad opportunities, challenges, and programs.

There's no definitive answer on how far ahead a strategic plan should look, but many organizations find that a three-year timeframe works well. If covering a longer timeframe, it becomes too reliant on predicting a future world that is likely to shift significantly. If covering a shorter period of time, it starts lacking a strategic feel and becomes more tactical in nature.

Ask a hundred nonprofit consultants how they would address strategic planning and you might get a hundred different approaches. Ask the same consultants how long it will take to create the plan and you will likewise get a range of answers. As mentioned, there is no right answer on how to go about strategic planning or how long it will take. We can, however, look at a strategic planning framework that could help your organization determine how long it will take for it to get to the strategic planning finish line.

Steps in a Strategic Planning Process

These six steps encompass a proven approach to moving through the key stages in a strategic planning process.

The Strategic Planning Process in Six Steps

1 Preparation	2 Stakeholder Feedback	3 Mission, Vision, Values
4 Goal Agreement	5 Drafting the Plan	6 Rolling Out the Plan

Figure 1.1. Summarization of the Strategic Planning Process

Step 1: Preparation

Before embarking on strategic planning, there are a few essential issues to consider. The first is ensuring that the board and staff agree with the time and resources necessary to invest in the process. Often, the impetus for strategic planning will come from the staff leadership, especially when there is a change in leadership. Other times, board members will desire to ensure a long-term plan is in place. Regardless of where the initial push comes from, it is vitally important that all parties are fully committed before this important work begins. In reality, focusing on strategic planning for a specific period of time means that other staff or board workstream(s) might need to take a back burner until the plan is completed.

The second consideration before starting a new strategic planning process is to decide who will be involved in it and at what stages. Having the entire board invested in the process is one thing, but having the whole board involved every step of the way is another.

One option is an inner circle or primary working group of four to five people, including staff leadership and a few board members, who have the bandwidth to meet at whatever cadence is needed to complete the process within your goal timeline. If you want to finalize a strategic plan in a reasonable amount of time (i.e., under six months), it will be extremely difficult to do so with a working group that incorporates the entire board, especially if the board comprises at least eight members. That said, gaining input and perspective from the whole board is possible and something I will touch on in the pages ahead.

A third matter to address upfront is to determine what information is going to be needed by the primary working group for them to do the work ahead. Gathering whatever data your organization currently collects on program costs and effectiveness, donor engagement and retention, marketing metrics, and anything else that is germane to your organization will expedite the process and help answer questions that will likely come up along the way. Having this data handy will allow the group to move from opinion-based decision making to information-based decision making.

The last and possibly most important issue to address prior to hitting the "go" button on strategic planning is whether your organization will need to bring in additional resources to help it navigate the process. Several factors could lead your organization in one direction or the other.

Whether to Bring in Outside Help for Strategic Planning

- Has someone on your team previously led a strategic planning process? Unless there is a board member or staff leader who has driven strategic planning in the past, embarking on this undertaking could be fraught with challenges if they are forced to learn on the job.

- Does your agency's strategic planning point person have the bandwidth to lead the process at this time? Even if they have the experience to do so, if their focus is elsewhere, strategic planning will suffer or drag on for longer than it should.

- Will having an internal team member leading the process inhibit their ability to participate? If they are facilitating or leading meetings, they may find themselves too wrapped up in that role to provide thoughtful input as key issues are being discussed.

- Do you think that having an outside voice or "accountability buddy" will be needed to keep the process on track? Sometimes, having someone else set up the meeting schedule and other logistics takes the Executive Director out of their usual role of herding the cats.

- Does your organization have the discretionary funds available to retain a consultant? Consultant fees for strategic planning could range wildly, but regardless of that range if you don't have the budget flexibility to absorb these fees, your options may be limited. Some financial solutions could be to engage pro-bono consultants, like Compass Pro Bono or PennPAC (you will learn more about those options in Chapter 13 when we discuss volunteer engagement) or seek a grant to underwrite the cost of retaining a consultant. That said, if you are taking the grant-funded route, there could be a significant time lag before those funds are secured.

- If you are intimidated by the notion of writing the strategic plan or lack clarity about a particular plan format, you may ultimately decide to bring in outside support to ensure that whatever is discussed throughout the process is committed to writing concisely and coherently. Sometimes, it is easier to be the editor than the originator for a document like a strategic plan.

Overall, there are a lot of decisions to consider at the initial stage. While addressing the considerations in the preparation phase of the process won't guarantee you come out with a successful strategic plan, it should increase the likelihood that your organization gets started on the right foot.

Step 2: Stakeholder Feedback and Synthesis

This second stage is one of the most critical in the entire process. Stakeholder feedback is where you identify which groups have experience and insights that could inform your strategic plan. For most organizations, these stakeholders include, but are not limited to, your staff, board, donors, clients, volunteers, strategic partners, and other relevant voices in your community.

Soliciting this feedback is not a one-size-fits-all proposition. In some cases, like with donors, it may be more appropriate to interview them one-on-one. In other cases, like with your staff, it may be helpful to organize an offsite meeting or retreat to give them space to reflect on the organization without the distractions that could interrupt a thoughtful deep dive into the issues at hand. With board members, a survey with a series of open-ended questions may be the best way to go. A survey of the entire board ensures that every board member has a voice in the early stages of the strategic planning process. An example of a brief board survey related to strategic planning is outlined below.

Sample Board Survey

- *Here is the organization's mission statement (include the mission statement word for word). Do you think this accurately reflects who we are? Are there any potential changes you think the organization should consider for its mission statement?*

- *What are the areas where you think _____ (name of organization) is particularly strong?*

- *What are two to three areas the organization needs to improve over the next few years to help achieve its mission?*

- *What opportunities, if pursued and developed, have the most potential for growth for our organization?*

- *What areas do you think represent the greatest threats to our organization?*

Ultimately, you are looking for patterns or trends from the feedback received. What are the common themes you keep hearing? Do the various groups have a similar set of insights regarding your organization? If so, that's good. Even if the news isn't good, consistency in what needs to be addressed can be extremely helpful.

Creating a SWOT Analysis

One tool that is particularly useful in terms of helping to synthesize this feedback is a SWOT analysis. A SWOT analysis will help you identify and group issues into strengths, weaknesses, opportunities, and threats. Your strategic plan could likely emerge from this short and organized list of topics. As you can see from the structure of the sample board survey above, you can develop tools that will help various stakeholders structure their feedback that easily translates into a SWOT analysis.

As indicated in the sample below, each quadrant of the SWOT analysis shouldn't replicate a laundry list of items. Ideally, you should identify the four to five highest priority items in each quadrant.

Strengths and weaknesses are internal facing and describe the organization in its current state. What does your organization currently do well or where is it deficient? What can be a source of sustainable competitive advantage? What gaps need to be filled to help your organization deliver on its mission? Assessing strengths and weaknesses involves an agency holding a mirror up to itself and being objective about both the good and the bad.

Conversely, opportunities and threats are external in nature. What opportunities if seized could propel your organization forward? What threats if not addressed could block organizational progress, or worse, cause it to go out of business?

Below is a version of the SWOT analysis depicting how a youth sports organization synthesized its stakeholder feedback. The purpose is to give you a sense for what the final output of a SWOT could look like.

SWOT Example: Youth Sports Organization

Strengths
- Quality of relationships/partners
- Proven track record
- Disaster relief niche
- Simplicity of the concept

Weaknesses
- Lack of fundraising muscle from Board
- Organizational structure still in infancy
- Lack of Board diversity
- Inability to measure impact

Opportunities
- Fully leveraging partnerships
- Board expansion
- Targeted awareness building
- Creating a resource development plan

Threats
- Growing competitor in Good Sports
- Poor relationship with MLBPA limits player engagement
- Cash on hand short term
- Financial strength long term

Figure 1.2. Sample SWOT Analysis

Step 3: Mission/Vision/Values

This step of the process is a significant opportunity to get everyone–board, staff, donors, and community–on the same page. (Re)gaining alignment on your organization's mission, vision, and values may be relatively straightforward, or it may be an opportunity to pivot or nuance some aspects of your organization.

Mission

When constructing the mission for your organization, seek simplicity and clarity. A mission should state why your organization exists, with an understanding of the anticipated theory of change that your organization is trying to accomplish among your target population. A straightforward way to do this with various stakeholders is to ask them:

1. Does our current mission statement appropriately represent who we are?

2. What changes would you make, if any?

3. This is another opportunity to look for patterns. If one major donor or board member thinks a change should be made, that shouldn't be enough to effect these kinds of fundamental decisions.

Vision

The organization's vision is a definition of what success looks like at some future point in time. In some cases, you can implement an approach focusing on what Jim Collins and Jerry Porras described as a Big Hairy Audacious Goal (BHAG) in their landmark book *Built to Last: Successful Habits of Visionary Companies*[3]. Vision statements should be simple and inspirational. Ultimately, if an organization were to achieve its vision it might render itself obsolete.

Sample Nonprofit Vision Statements

- Alzheimer's Association: A world without Alzheimer's.

- The Nature Conservancy: To leave a sustainable world for future generations.

- Cleveland Clinic: Striving to be the world's leader in patient experience, clinical outcomes, research, and education.

- Save the Children: A world in which every child attains the right to survival, protection, development, and participation.

---

[3] Jim Collins and Jerry I. Porras, Built To Last: Successful Habits of Visionary Companies (New York: Harper Business, 1994), n.p.

- Teach for America: One day, all children in this nation will have the opportunity to attain an excellent education.

- World Wildlife Fund: We seek to save a planet, a world of life. Reconciling the needs of human beings and the needs of others that share the earth.

- Kiva: We envision a world where all people – even in the most remote areas of the globe – hold the power to create opportunity for themselves and others.

Values

A values statement is a commitment to how you want to operate. It's a way of articulating the culture you seek to create for your internal team, the constituents you serve, and your various stakeholder groups. Below is an example of a well-thought-out values statement.

Sample values statement: Amnesty International

- <u>Accountable</u>: Consistently striving to reach your goals in a thorough, timely way that you can be proud of, and re-empowering others to do the same.

- <u>Considerate</u>: Support your colleagues and try to find out what motivates them to do their best, and what pressures they are under so that you can consider this when you work together.

- <u>Creative</u>: Continuously looking for new and innovative solutions and encouraging others' ideas so that we can adapt and succeed in an ever-changing and uncertain global environment.

- <u>Decisive</u>: Making sound judgments within your work so that a project or activity can progress with pace and confidence.

- <u>Respectful</u>: Treat your colleagues with equality and dignity and assume they have integrity. Value your colleagues' perspectives and show them their contributions and expertise matter.

Step 4: Goal Agreement

When you reach step four, you have reached the guts of the strategic planning process. This step is where the most critical decisions will be made. Effectively, your organization is betting on where it wants to go and how it plans to get there over the next few years.

Goal agreement means identifying the three to four key areas where resources will be allocated to make the most significant impact on the organization over the long term. Before we identify some examples of goal setting, let's cover the ground rules for good goal setting. SMART is an acronym that describes the elements of a well-defined goal. Well-articulated goals are specific, measurable, achievable, relevant, and time-bound. For example, the goal of "building awareness for your organization" lacks specificity, measurability, and a time component. In contrast, wanting to "build web traffic by 40% over the next two years" might be a specific and measurable way of accomplishing the same goal for your organization.

Another example of an insufficient goal would be to "grow our board of directors", while a more thorough and comprehensive goal statement might be to "increase our board of directors to 15 within three years." In the first case, you have not defined success clearly enough. How much growth is needed and by when? In the latter case, you know exactly what success looks like and when and can design a plan to help you get from your current state to where you want to be.

Which goals are suitable for your organization? Only you and your inner circle of staff and board leadership can determine that. Every organization is different in terms of its needs, opportunities, and vulnerabilities. However, what you and your decision-makers need to demonstrate in this section is the discipline to identify those top three to four goals that are achievable by your organization given your staff and anticipated budget resources. While this selection of the "right" goals may be a challenging exercise, it is essential. Choose goals that are too narrow and you may reach them without changing the trajectory of your organization or achieving a meaningful target. Choose goals that are too far-reaching and you are setting your team up for failure and frustration. Choose too many goals, and you will spread your team too thin to see them all the way through to completion.

Step 5: Drafting the Plan

Once the broader measurable goals have been identified, the challenge will be to craft strategies and tactical plans to reach them. The level of detail in terms of tactics, budgets, and who will be responsible for various aspects of these plans will be critical to creating accountability as the plan moves forward. As the expression goes, "the devil is in the details", and strategic plans are no different. Strategies with dates, forecasted budgets, and clear milestones will help your plan go from paper to reality.

There is no correct format for the drafting of a strategic plan. Here is a sample framework that I have seen frequently utilized.

- **Letter from the CEO or Board President**: This is a brief introduction to the strategic plan and gives an overview of the process used in crafting it. The primary purpose of the letter is to express gratitude for the work involved and to create excitement and motivation for the reader.

- **Executive Summary**: Many readers may not want to invest the time to read the entire plan. The executive summary is a synopsis of the highlights contained within the plan. It should be no longer than half a page.

- **State of the Organization**: This section includes the mission/vision/values and describes how the organization performs against its mission. In addition, highlight signature programs and other strengths of the organization. You could also reference the current state of your board, your budget, and other critical aspects of your operation. This section intends to give the reader a sense of the organization's current position before seeing what lies ahead in the strategic plan.

- **Strategic priorities**: Outline the three to four primary goals your organization intends to address throughout the strategic plan. This not only states the broader goals but also clearly outlines the strategies and tactics that you envision will be employed to achieve these respective goals.

- **Financial projections**: As your organization moves into the future, your plan should convey how your budget will evolve to meet the goals and challenges you have outlined.

- **Appendices:** This section is where you share your detailed tactical plans identifying individuals responsible for each component and when they are expected to be completed.

Once a draft of the plan is created, seek feedback from staff and board members to help gain further alignment and buy-in to the plan. While the primary work group will be the ones making the document, the entire organization needs to be on board before the plan becomes finalized.

Step 6: Rolling Out the Plan

Once your team has agreed upon a plan, it must make critical communications and operational decisions. From a communications perspective, you are now in a position to share the plan with staff, strategic partners, and your broader community of supporters and volunteers. Just because you have been working on this plan for many months does not mean others will naturally understand the significance of focusing the organization's resources in a particular manner. Sharing a condensed version of your plan (without the financials and detailed tactical plans) on social media, on your website, and in one-on-one meetings with major donors and stakeholders is a chance to increase their sense of commitment to the organization and its future, creating an opportunity to describe the clear vision of what lies ahead and why the organization will be more effective once these plans are executed.

Operationally, most organizations can't do everything all at once. Remember, this is likely a three-year plan. Having a thoughtful approach to which planks of the plan will be addressed by which departments and in what order is critical. Rome wasn't built in a day and your team won't be able to implement the myriad of strategies and plans all at once. This strategic plan is more of a marathon than a sprint. Discipline will be your friend in terms of setting expectations for how much can be achieved over the first 6-12 months of your multi-year plan.

Another critical element of rolling out your plan is the ability to utilize it as a means to galvanize fundraising efforts. When distilled in this fashion, your condensed strategic plan is effectively the organization's elevator pitch: this is who we are and what we plan to accomplish soon. It is likely that some aspects of your plan will require additional resources. Laying out a clear vision for the future and how resources will be deployed to achieve meaningful change for your agency can be an essential marketing tool. This represents an opportunity to engage board members, major donors, and potential grant funders to help secure the funds needed to implement your plan.

Summary

Ben Franklin is credited with saying, "If you are failing to plan, you are planning to fail." As discussed above, strategic planning doesn't need to be a drawn out and painful process. The act of writing a concise plan can bring the organization together and give it a sense of common purpose. Strategic planning can put all key stakeholders on the same page and focus resources and plans to bring an organization to greater heights. In contrast, not having an effective plan creates an environment where short term circumstances or individual key players can cause an organization to veer off course or chase fanciful opportunities. While there is no shortage of approaches to strategic planning, committing to one and getting the organization's best thinking onto paper will yield positive outcomes more often than not.

Actionable Next Steps

1. Ensure that leadership and key stakeholders agree on the need for strategic planning and are ready to provide the necessary resources.

2. Conduct an honest assessment of whether an outside consultant will be needed and what the budget would be to hire one.

3. Choose a diverse group of board members and staff to lead the strategic planning efforts.

4. Identify the types of data and information needed to inform the planning process, such as financial records and performance metrics.

5. Decide how you will gather feedback from stakeholders, choosing appropriate methods like surveys or interviews.

CHAPTER 2:
Building Your Board

Chapter Overview: *This chapter addresses the common challenges that many nonprofit leaders face regarding the Board of Directors, its critical roles and responsibilities, and offers practical tips to help recruit new members.*

A board is a living breathing entity. It's a community. In some cases, it's a family, albeit a dysfunctional one. Communities and families have norms, accepted behaviors, a way of doing things.

You want a board that is active, engaged, responsive, generous, and committed. The big question is how to achieve these characteristics, rather than the more common ones associated with boards: quiet, unavailable, unwilling, and checked out.

There is no more common mantra from nonprofit CEOs than "my board is a mess." That phrase can mean a range of things, but it tends to fall into the following buckets:

- My board doesn't engage.

- Our board meetings last up to three hours and we never get anything done.

- My board doesn't fundraise.

- We have trouble finding new board members.

- My board doesn't understand their role in the organization.

- Our board doesn't really have productive committees.

Let's look at these one at a time.

Lack of Board Engagement

Here's the typical scenario. The nonprofit CEO runs the board meeting. They report on various initiatives and program elements. The board sits there nodding respectfully, even enthusiastically. They don't ask questions. They likely haven't read the board packet in advance of the meeting. There may be an ask of the board but the CEO knows in their heart that board members individually and collectively won't do what is being asked of them.

Many agency leaders inherit a board where many members have been on for over 20 years. In other cases, board members simply don't show up, respond to emails, or meet the commitments they make in the presence of others at regular meetings.

If this doesn't sound familiar, consider yourself fortunate. If it does, read on. In my experience, this lethargy and lack of commitment comes from not setting clear expectations upfront for what board service entails. Without a clear set of expectations, it is much harder to expect accountability for their actions (or inaction) once they become a board member.

So, how do you set expectations to increase the likelihood that a board member will perform as hoped? During my tenure as CEO, I adopted a more rigorous vetting process. Prospective board members received a list of roles and responsibilities that detailed what would be expected of them. These expectations included the following:

Attending meetings throughout the year

Participating on a board committee

Attending the annual board retreat

Meeting a fundraising *give/get* target annually[4]

Setting the strategy for the organization

Evaluating the CEO

Overseeing the financial condition of the organization

Trying to identify new opportunities for the organization

This document was sent to them early in the recruiting process in advance of a call with either a current board member

---

4   A give/get policy is a requirement that all directors on the organization's board either "give" and/or "get" a certain fundraising goal for the organization. For organizations with a "give or get" policy, each director can either donate the required amount or raise the desired amount through fundraising activities.

or the Executive Director. The purpose of that call was to methodically walk through the key board responsibilities and related time commitment to ensure they were understood and to get a sense for their potential role within the organization. Before someone can make an intelligent decision regarding board service, they should know what is expected of them. It's basic adult behavior.

Before the call concludes, and based on their experience and skill set, it is entirely fair to ask where they see themselves making a difference initially. Lastly, in addition to clarifying up front what was expected of them, board members were told that they would be evaluated annually on the items articulated in this roles and expectations document.

The goal of the annual evaluation isn't to embarrass anyone. It is to let them know that board service is an important volunteer assignment and that the board members feel it is important to hold each other accountable.

Don't get me wrong; I didn't always operate this way, and the results showed. My first few boards had a distinct friends and family feel to them. We were fantastic at having fun but not so great at getting results.

So what changed? Everything.

First of all, we stopped conducting board meetings as a review of what was going on within the organization. This was much more efficiently accomplished with a detailed program report reviewing the recent happenings within the agency since the last board meeting. Many boards achieve this with what is called a *consent agenda*[5]. Since this review doesn't require significant board action, finding a way to share this information outside of the board meeting helps free up time for more pressing matters.

Second, we started shifting the board's time and focus away from programming and onto strategy. Where did the organization want to go? What would it take to get there? Focusing the board on the future was much more important and motivating than understanding the here and now. If you don't want your board in the weeds of basic operations, don't spend your entire board meeting talking about the day-to-day challenges you are facing.

Third, we started asking more probing questions that board members had to respond to in our meetings. They were informed beforehand of the topics/questions that would be discussed and asked to come to the meeting with input or questions related to those topics. After the issues are presented during the meeting, you can say, "Let's go around the table and share our thoughts. Who wants to get us started?" It sounds simplistic, but it works.

Finally, we changed the profile of who we were looking for as a potential board member. Philosophically, we wanted our board to be a capacity-building board and not a working board. In simplest terms, a capacity-building board is expected to take an active role in bringing in new resources and opening up doors to new opportunities.

---

5   A consent agenda, also known as a "consent calendar" in Robert's Rule of Order, refers to individual points of discussion that are bundled into a single action item. A key advantage of consent agenda is that it allows a board to approve all actions with one single motion instead of filing multiple motions.

A working board is a different model. In this approach, board members are expected to contribute functional expertise (accounting, marketing, legal support, clinical knowledge etc.). If your board is a working board, that is fine. You just need to set those expectations up front and hold members accountable to make sure they are holding up their end of the deal.

At the end of the day, the keys to greater board engagement were 1) shifting the focus of the regular meetings away from current programming to a more forward-thinking and strategic lens; and 2) making sure board members knew what was expected of them and instituting a process to track their performance.

Our Board Meetings Are Too Long and Unproductive

Running timely meetings is all about respecting people's time. I never ran a meeting for more than 90 minutes. Just because a board member (or a CEO) loves the sound of their own voice, doesn't mean that everyone else has to serve as their audience. While I did believe strongly in having an annual board retreat, our regular meetings were started on time and finished on time. Once you have instituted a consent agenda or a program report you have cleared the way to focus on those matters that require board input or give board committees the opportunity to cover in some depth what they are working on.

Board members will always offer ideas. Some of them may even be helpful. However, when the conversation gravitates too far away from the published agenda and towards being hijacked, either the CEO or the Board President has to assert themselves. Board members can be assured that you will follow up with them outside of the meeting to understand their ideas or concerns better, but it is critical to sense when things are moving in the wrong direction and to course correct as soon as possible.

Ultimately, most of the critical conversations I've ever had with board members were one-on-one anyway. Board members need to approve budgets, vote on a new slate of board members, discuss the CEO evaluation and compensation, understand where the organization is in terms of finances, and many other critical matters. Keeping board members from derailing meetings is a shared responsibility. Talk about it openly. Talk about the discipline to stay on the agenda with the comfort that you and the Board President are available any time to discuss other issues.

My Board Doesn't Fundraise

This is an oldie but a goodie. It is rare to find a board where everyone rises to the challenge and meets their give/get obligations. Why does this happen so often? In my judgment, it goes back to the vetting process.

- How openly did you discuss their give/get target before they joined the board?

- How much did you probe their prior nonprofit board experience and performance?

- Did you ask them how they might feel about engaging members of their personal and professional networks to benefit the organization financially?

Most prospective board members will give you clues as to their comfort level regarding fundraising. Pay attention to the answers to these questions and ask as many follow-up questions as needed. The time to gain a better understanding of their experience and willingness to be an active fundraiser is before they join your organization, not after.

It's ok to let the prospective board member know that there are many things that you hope they can achieve for the organization, not just being a source of revenue. It is also ok, however, to let a prospect know that the fundraising topic is the one that tends to create the most friction for the organization and that is why you are going to focus on it up front. If you are intent on a capacity-building board, the time to deal with these matters is before someone joins.

Each board member may have a very different vision of how they can best help the organization access funding. It's therefore critical to create a flexible funding mindset when working with your board. Sure, you may have an annual gala and all board members may be asked to purchase/sell a certain number of tickets. In the end, however, a true give/get fundraising strategy implies that the organization doesn't really care how the board member hits their fundraising target, just that they hit it. Our job as staff leadership is to engage them on the topic, try to identify what element of your mission or program resonates with them, and build a fundraising game plan around that.

Some board members may tackle development the old-fashioned way. They may simply write a check and be done with it. Others may have a broad network and engage them through peer-to-peer fundraising[6]. Others may target a few high-net-

---

6   Peer-to-peer fundraising is a fundraising method in which individual supporters host personalized campaigns to collect donations from friends, family, and colleagues on behalf of your nonprofit.

worth individuals to join or match their gifts. There are lots of ways to hit a fundraising goal. It is essential to "meet board members where they are" and develop a plan that meets their comfort level, experience base, and time demands.

I Can't Find New Board Members

Most nonprofit leaders spend considerable time and energy asking their board members to identify additional board prospects. Usually, this exercise is only marginally productive. As a group, board members don't whiteboard things well. What I mean by this is they are better at responding to a specific request than responding to something open-ended. "Do you know anyone who might be a good addition to our board?" is sometimes less helpful than "Do you know any senior executives in this particular sector or from this specific geographic location?"

One approach many boards take in thinking about new members is to conduct a gap analysis. Are there certain traits or characteristics that the board is seeking? If so, which ones are covered sufficiently, and which ones are not? Some examples of gaps or needs might be looking for candidates with a legal, accounting or marketing background, a certain racial background, or possibly a certain geography. The question then becomes something like, "Do you know a lawyer you think might be a good candidate?" Or, "Do you know someone from California who might be a good candidate?" This kind of specific prompt will likely yield much better results than broadly or generally asking board members if they know anyone who might be a good fit.

Another useful approach is to develop a profile of an ideal board member. Let's say you are involved with an organization like Row New York. This is an organization that utilizes the discipline of rowing and rigorous academic support to transform the lives of New Yorkers. If I was in charge of helping them identify new prospective board members, I would suggest they should look for New York-based executives who rowed in college. These folks would likely have a passion for the mission, care about making a difference in their community, and have resources and networks that could positively impact the revenue goals of the organization.

So how do you find them? Let's come up with a game plan.

1. You can scour LinkedIn and filter whatever search terms you think are applicable. Let the internet go to work for you.

2. You can post on your personal LinkedIn or Facebook pages that your organization is seeking new board candidates and see who may self-identify or may know of someone fitting the profile you are seeking.

3. You can identify if there are private rowing clubs in NY (there are). In this case, you could find out if the club had events or communication pieces where you could get the word out that your rowing-centric nonprofit is looking to grow its board.

4. There are placement/matching services that will help locate board members for a fee. These services can filter your match based on geography, areas of interest, and

financial requirements of your agency. (See a list of these services in actionable next steps at the end of the chapter).

5. You can post board member positions on platforms like Indeed or Idealist or other job boards with a description of the ideal candidate.

6. You make it a point of asking people you meet if they know of people fitting the desired characteristics. As the old adage goes, "If you don't ask, you don't get."

Now just because you find a qualified candidate doesn't mean you are going to be able to land the fish into the boat. Cultivating candidates is a process that requires planning, patience, and discipline.

In the end, you want to get the board prospect excited about the organization. How do you do that? Invite them to your fundraising events, volunteer opportunities, or where your programs are delivered. Share success stories. Ask current board members to participate in the recruitment process. Schedule calls. Take them to lunch. Sell them on the impact that the organization is making. None of this is rocket science but it does all take time, planning, and effort.

Some organizations will meet someone and immediately want to consider inviting them to join the board. Certainly, this can work, but it is fraught with trouble.

- Is it too easy to join your board?

- Shouldn't there be some effort involved in joining?

- Does the candidate even know what is expected of them in terms of time, financial support, and engagement?

Filling board seats with qualified candidates takes time and discipline. For many nonprofit CEOs, building the board you desire is one of the most important investments of time you can make. Don't complain about a board not performing. Help fix it!

My Board Doesn't Know What Their Role Is

Board governance refers to the systems, rules, and processes by which a nonprofit organization is directed and controlled. The board, not the staff leadership, is ultimately responsible for overseeing the organization's activities, ensuring it fulfills its mission, and managing its resources responsibly. This governance structure helps ensure that the agency operates effectively and transparently, adheres to legal and ethical standards, and works towards achieving its goals.

Sharmila Rao Thakkar is a former nonprofit Executive Director and a terrific nonprofit consultant and coach. A big focus of her practice is board governance and training. "Good governance allows sustainability. It allows organizations to be effective and efficient and achieve their goals not only today but into the future."

In her experience, the nonprofits that had intentional, responsive, and well-trained boards were the organizations that not only survived the pandemic, but thrived. They strengthened or tweaked their missions, reimagined their programming to meet the ever-changing needs of the moment, brought in new donors, and grew the populations of individuals they served.

Sharmila helps identify five pillars of governance with her clients. "Everything a board does is governance. Mission and vision alignment. Program integrity. Risk management. Financial management. This is all part of effective governance."

WHAT IS GOVERNANCE?

Governance is the process of ensuring a nonprofit's mission integrity, program integrity, ethical integrity, financial integrity, and legal compliance. It entails policy making, strategic planning, long-term vision, and evaluating performance.

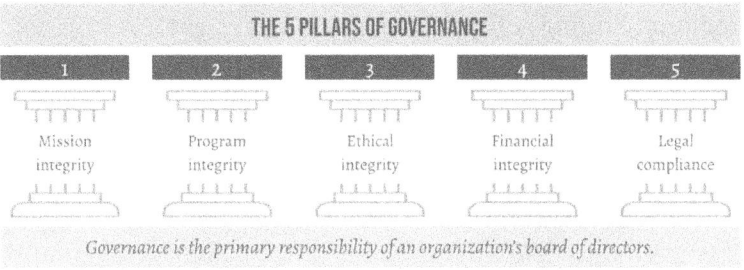

Governance is the primary responsibility of an organization's board of directors.

Figure 2.1. Sharmila Rao Thakkar's Five Pillars of Governance

Sharmila observes that ineffective boards tend not to be fully connected to the organization. "Passion for the mission of an organization is not enough. Even if board members have passion and skills, it doesn't guarantee they will know how to effectively use them for the organization's benefit. It's essential to onboard and train board members so they understand how to contribute effectively. One thing that is often missing with ineffective boards is the simple notion of not having a position description for board members and a clear path for them to co-craft and meet expectations." When we put as much care into training a board member and incorporating periodic check-ins as we do with a new member of our staff, we often see a difference in engagement—something we hear nonprofits often struggle with.

Too often we expect our board members to be able to just jump into their work, knowing what, when, and how to get things done. Where boards should start based on Sharmila's experience is making sure there is alignment between the organization's mission and vision. Beyond that, boards should address the organization's core values, guiding principles, programs and operations, including financials. It's important to remember that even if an organization has its mission, vision, and values articulated, because of turnover many board members might not have been part of the process of establishing them. An annual or bi-annual board refresh can do wonders in providing an opportunity for board members and staff to revisit priorities and expectations, re-energize and get on the same page about roles and responsibilities given the organization's life stage and current strategy.

Board Committees

One area where boards vary widely is in their use of committees. Committees are a common and practical way to handle a task on the board's agenda, providing focus and advice on a particular workstream of the organization. Their role is to help structure and manage the board's work. Effective committees have clearly defined responsibilities. This can start with something as basic as a charter or objective of the committee. It is unusual for a board to give decision-making authority to a committee. In most cases, its recommendations still need to be approved by the full board.

Some organizations may have committees outlined in their bylaws. If that is the case, these committees are what are referred to as "standing" committees. Many boards require each board member to serve on at least one committee in addition to their role on the Board of Directors. The most common standing committees are finance, fundraising, governance/nominating, and executive.

- **Finance committee**: This committee would typically be responsible for the audit process, interacting with whoever is preparing the organization's 990 (your agency's annual federal tax return), the creation of the annual budget, making sure there are sound internal controls as relates to the handling of funds, and ongoing reporting as relates to cash flow. Many organizations have a treasurer and they along with the Executive Director and other board members would populate this committee.

- **Fundraising committee**: This committee would be taking the lead on helping the organization create and then achieve its fundraising goals. While the Board President and the director of development are often on this committee, anyone can serve on this committee. Many organizations will often recruit non-board members to serve on the development committee as a way to increase the reach of the organization and as a pipeline for future members. While development may be a standing committee, many organizations will often form ad hoc committees, especially around things like fundraising galas and other special events.

- **Governance/nominating**: While we discussed governance in broad terms above, this committee may have specific responsibilities to ensure that the organization's bylaws are up to date or that the organization is in compliance in regard to matters like conflict of interest and other policies. Nominations of new board members typically flow through this committee. Having an established process to vet and onboard new board members is a key area of focus for this committee in many cases.

- **Executive**: This committee is responsible for the hiring and evaluating of the Executive Director. They also will review and make recommendations related to the compensation of the staff leadership. As articulated in the bylaws, the executive committee can have the authority to act on behalf of the board between regular meetings and is the group that is normally assembled in a crisis or urgent situations.

There are countless iterations of committee structures and no one structure is the right one. Each organization should right-size its structure based on its current and anticipated needs.

Summary

While dealing with boards can be an enormous source of frustration, it doesn't need to be. A high-performing board can be a source of long-term growth and opportunity for almost any nonprofit. Nurturing and developing your board is a mission-critical endeavor and one that can pay huge dividends in the short and long term. Bring in the right people with clear expectations. Respect their time and talents. Engage them in meaningful work and hold them accountable. Partner with them to build a culture of action and optimism. If you do, the sky's the limit.

Actionable Next Steps

1. Draft a roles and expectations document for prospective board members. If you don't have one of these for your organization or want to review what you currently have on this subject, scan this QR code to book some time on my calendar and I can share an example with you. This conversation won't cost you anything.

2. Discuss the concept of yearly board member evaluations with your Board President to get feedback on how this might be received within your group.

3. Consider using a consent agenda or program report for your next board meeting to create more time for strategic conversations.

4. Initiate a gap analysis to identify what skills your board lacks and to prioritize new members who can fill these gaps.

5. Investigate one of these board matching/placement services to see if they are a good fit for your organization's needs. Some options include BoardAssist, BoardStrong, BoardSource, DiverseForce, Board Member Connect, and Center for Nonprofit Advancement Board Match Program.

CHAPTER 3:
Building Your Fundraising Strategy

Chapter Overview: This chapter illustrates the various ways a nonprofit organization can attract financial support and provides considerations and strategies for success within these different revenue streams.

Financial resources are the fuel that drive every organization. You might have the greatest mission and some really well thought out programs, but without the right resources even your best laid plans won't ever get off the ground.

You may be aware of the game "Six Degrees of Kevin Bacon". It refers to the notion that you can trace everyone in Hollywood back to actor Kevin Bacon within six points of connection.

For nonprofits, I think of fundraising as one degree of separation. Meaning, if you aren't directly involved with fundraising then it's unlikely that you are more than one step away from the work you are doing playing a major role in fundraising.

- Our communications directly tie to fundraising. This is where we build our community and share our successes that might ultimately motivate someone to donate.

- Our programs are where we are making a difference. It is the lives we are changing that become the source of stories that embody the impact and reach of our organization.

- Our measurement and evaluation help articulate and demonstrate the difference we are making with the populations we are serving.

- Volunteers engage directly with our programs. They can oftentimes be the eyes and ears to the stories we want to highlight, often becoming some of our strongest advocates. Because of their demonstrated commitment to the organization, volunteers can often be a source of fundraising success.

The Fundraising Landscape

According to CCS Fundraising, one of the leading nonprofit fundraising consultancies in the United States, annual philanthropic giving in the United States totaled about $500 million in 2022[7]. This marked a slight decrease from the prior two years, when charitable giving peaked in response to the global pandemic. Giving from foundations, donor advised funds (DAFs), and bequests increased slightly while donations from individuals and corporations, as well as overall number of donors, all decreased.

---

7   CCS Fundraising, 2023 Philanthropic Landscape, 12th Edition: 3

Many people believe (or hope) that because the focus of the nonprofit sector is supposed to be mission-driven, rather than profit-driven, that this sector of the economy must be less competitive than others. But there are around 1.8 million nonprofit organizations in the United States alone and to a certain degree they are all competing for the same philanthropic dollars[8]. So don't kid yourself, fundraising is a contact sport.

Eileen Heisman has had the opportunity to assess the fundraising landscape from her position as the CEO of the National Philanthropic Trust (NPT) for over twenty-five years. A few trends that Eileen has noticed include:

1. "With the continued concentration of wealth in high-net-worth individuals and families, organizations need to be really good at cultivating and attracting major gifts. Figuring out how to navigate that world can be really intimidating to small and mid-sized nonprofits".

2. Eileen sees a continued trend and importance with Donor Advised Funds (DAFs). "I started working with DAFs in 1987. Today, they are an increasingly large part of how people choose to support causes. At NPT, the smallest grant a donor can recommend is $250. In the past, someone may have recommended only a $50 or $100 grant. Now, in NPT's case, donors make a minimum grant of $250. That can add up".

3. Contrary to recent claims, Eileen doesn't think that younger donors are very different from the prior

---

[8] Urban Institute, 2021

generation of donors. "Every new generation embraces similar principles than the previous, often using different nomenclature for similar actions and intentions. Every generation I've worked with for over 30 years has wanted to know the impact of their gift. Younger people are just as interested in seeing that impact as their grandparents were. The differences today are the tools and technology available to both receive information about charitable interests and how to support them".

The Revenue Pie

Before we dive headfirst into fundraising, it is important to have a clear understanding of the various potential sources of financial support and how they stack up against each other. As the pie chart below shows, about 2/3 of all charitable giving comes from individuals. This key figure is often shocking to many nonprofit leaders and board members. They imagine that charitable foundations or big corporations dominate the fundraising landscape. But as you can see, foundations and corporations only represent 21% and 6% of the fundraising world respectively.

Chapter 3: Building Your Fundraising Strategy

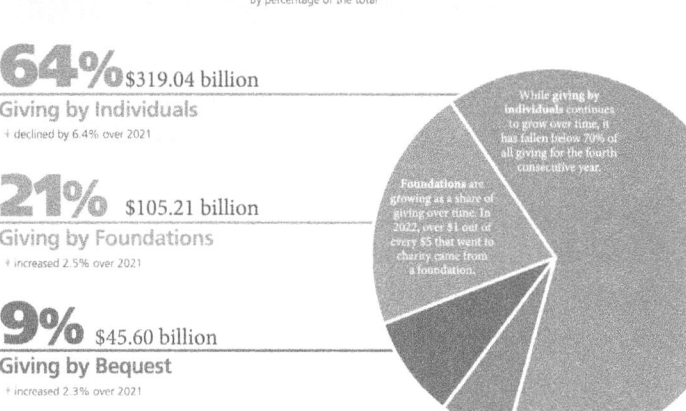

Figure 3.1. Philanthropic giving by source; Giving USA Foundation, 2023

Individual Giving

In the war room of Bill Clinton's presidential campaign strategy, there was reportedly a sign that said "It's the economy, stupid!" Given that the majority of philanthropic giving comes from individual donors, maybe resource development staff offices should have a comparable sign that says "It's individual donors, stupid!" It is crucial that the primary focus of any resource development plan should be to make sure that this segment of your donor audience is being addressed with intention and a clear strategy.

There are a number of reasons that individuals make charitable gifts. A recent study by Donor Box revealed that for 97% of donors, their primary motivator for giving is seeing the impact that their gift is making, while 56% of donors list the tax advantages of making a donation as being important[9]. The implication of the above is that both factors are relevant and that is why over 47% of online giving takes place in the month of December just prior to the close of the tax year.

A trend that Elizabeth Abel, a senior vice president at CCS Fundraising, has observed is that the traditional annual campaign, the staple of many nonprofit fundraising efforts, continues to evolve. Historically, nonprofits would reach out to all prior donors with one signature campaign a year that would hopefully motivate them to give again to the organization. Now there simply isn't just one annual campaign anymore. Organizations might have four or more campaigns throughout the year.

One event which has grown in significance in recent years is Giving Tuesday. Giving Tuesday is the Tuesday after Thanksgiving each year and has become a rallying cry for most nonprofit organizations in the United States. According to the same Donor Box study cited above, $3.1 billion dollars were donated collectively through Giving Tuesday campaigns in 2022, representing about 4% of year-end online giving. So while Giving Tuesday gets a lot of hype and is worth building a campaign for, it isn't a silver bullet that can solve your fundraising goals. Giving Tuesday is crowded, if not overwhelming, so from a consumer perspective, the proliferation of emails during this period is likely causing significant donor fatigue.

---

9   "18 Year-End Giving Statistics with Surprising Facts [2023]", Kristine Ensor, donorboxBlog, October 6, 2023, https://donorbox.org/nonprofit-blog/end-of-year-giving-statistics

For Elizabeth Abel, "the best indicator of future fundraising success is an analysis of previous fundraising performance. Is your fundraising increasing or decreasing over the last three to five years, and how does that break down by key giving levels? Has your pool of major donors changed?"

Elizabeth's client involvement shapes her belief that the key is and will remain individuals who make major gifts. "As we help clients think about their fundraising, and from my experience, over 80% of individual gifts come from roughly 20% of donors. And if anything, the concentration of individual giving is skewing more towards major gifts."

The definition of what constitutes a "major" gift will differ for each organization based on their overall budget and the make up of its donor base. Regardless of the actual size of the donation, major gifts are all about relationships and making a connection with the individual donor. One of the critical roles that a Board of Directors can play is to be a pathway to meet and engage potential major donors. Many board members may need significant training and support before they can confidently start connecting you to people in their networks, but it's their willingness to help you identify those donor prospects that is the most important element for success in that role.

This can also work in reverse. An organization may identify potential influential donors and then ask board members to see who within the organization may have a direct or indirect relationship with these prospects. Relationship mapping platforms are another relatively new piece of technology that can assist with identifying who within your organization can help you connect with prospects you have identified[10]. Relationship mapping platforms can vary in terms of their annual costs, but they can also easily pay for themselves with the first major gift that they help the agency obtain.

Regardless of how you get connected with them, it is important to understand that engaging major donors, unlike grassroots or smaller donors, is a process. And this process will likely take time and involve a series of carefully calculated steps.

In the nonprofit sector, the journey to attract people who care and ultimately donate to an organization includes the following key phases:

- **Awareness:** People are not going to make a gift to an organization until they are familiar with the work it is doing and the impact it is making. In the best case scenario, this initial awareness-building phase takes place in a one-on-one conversation where you begin to paint a picture of how your organization is impacting the community and share your vision for future growth. However if a one-on-one conversation isn't an option, you can help create this awareness via digital marketing or social media, encouraging the prospect to become involved as a volunteer, or inviting them to attend other events that the organization is conducting.

- **Consideration:** In the case of a major donor, there is a point where they formally or informally start listing out

---

10   Relationship mapping is a tool for nonprofits to identify and cultivate potential donors. It involves creating a visual representation of the connections between your organization, your existing supporters, and your donor prospects.

the organizations that they are giving consideration to and begin the process of making decisions about which organizations to support and to what extent. Many major donors have set budgets and funding guidelines that drive their ultimate allocation of charitable dollars. It is your role as a development officer of the agency to learn about what motivates them to make philanthropic decisions and when these decisions get made.

- **Conversion:** This is where a prospect becomes part of your community by making a donation. Donors don't typically make a meaningful financial contribution unless they are asked, and there is both an art and a science to determining when to make the ask, who should be making the ask, and how much you should be asking for.

- **Retention:** Once someone has made their first gift, a stewardship process needs to take place. The goal of this stewardship is to keep them connected to your work and for them to make a habit of supporting your agency annually. Ideally, you can motivate them to increase the size of their gift over time (known as moves management). At its core, stewardship is recognizing and appreciating the donor's generosity and sharing with them how their gift is helping to make an impact on the constituents you are trying to serve.

- **Advocacy:** Ultimately, your major donors can become your biggest cheerleaders and hopefully serve as a magnet to attract additional resources. If someone finds out about a great restaurant or reads a great book, they tell their friends. The same can happen when someone becomes a true believer in the work your organization is doing. You can facilitate donors into becoming advocates by providing them with talking points or anecdotes that capture your agency's impact on constituents who participate in your programs. Armed with this information, current donors can share this information with members of their network and hopefully attract others to your community of supporters.

Each of these phases requires thoughtful strategy, time, resources, and execution. Successful fundraising isn't luck. It takes people and planning to maintain and grow your individual donor base.

Figure 3.2. Steps to Attracting Donors in the Nonprofit Sector

Capital Campaigns

Capital campaigns are fundraising initiatives typically aimed at funding a major new asset for your organization, such as a new building. Unlike annual resource development planning, capital campaigns have a time horizon which typically extends several years. It is not uncommon for nonprofits to engage outside consulting support to help them assess the feasibility of raising this kind of capital. Fundraising consultants will often need to educate agencies on some of the differences between the kinds of fundraising they typically do with the dynamics that will likely be present with a capital campaign. Capital campaigns will often involve new strategies and approaches to attracting major donors to fund large organizational investments. Consultants can help with the development of the marketing materials needed to support donor outreach for these campaigns.

Kenny Holdsman is the Chief Executive Officer and Co-Founder of Philadelphia Youth Basketball (PYB). PYB uses the iconic game of basketball to deliver life-changing opportunities and experiences. Built of, by, for, and with the communities we serve, PYB provides a safe, nurturing environment for young people to build the skill-sets and mindsets they need to succeed on the court and in their education, careers, and lives. I have known Kenny for over 20 years. He is one of the brightest minds I have met in the nonprofit sector.

The centerpiece of PYB's programmatic work is their 100,000-square-foot educational and basketball facility, known as The Alan Horwitz "Sixth Man Center." More on the name and its significance soon.

In the months after PYB launched its $25 million capital campaign to fund the construction of the center they were having some early fundraising success. They had commitments for just under $2 million, but they had a long way to go. One day, Kenny was at the gym, really struggling due to the recent tragic death of one of PYB's beloved Coach-Mentors - a death that left behind that Coach-Mentor's 12-year-old son and daughter. So when a friend innocently asked Kenny how he was doing the day after the tragedy, he responded honestly with "not well" and conveyed this devastating story. His friend acknowledged the sad account and asked Kenny to hold on while he made a call. This call eventually transformed the capital campaign and the future of the organization.

The person the friend contacted was Alan Horwitz, an extremely successful and respected real estate developer in Philadelphia. Alan Horwitz is also a fixture at Philadelphia 76ers basketball games. He has courtside seats next to the players and coaches at every home game. Because of this very visible location and his exuberant support of the team, Alan is affectionately known as the team's "sixth man" by other fans and the team's announcers.

Over the next several days, Alan Horwitz invited the Coach-Mentor's 12 year old son and his immediate family to accompany him at 76ers and Eagles games. During this same period of time, the relationship between Kenny and Alan developed as did Alan's awareness of what PYB was trying to accomplish in the community. Given this growing relationship, Kenny asked David Adelman, the business partner of Alan Horwitz, if there was something more to Alan's connection to PYB and this family.

David Adelman revealed to Kenny that, like the young man in this tragedy, Alan also lost his father at a very young age.

In the end, Alan made a $5,000,000 commitment to PYB's capital campaign. Having a leadership gift of this level from someone so well respected in the Philadelphia business and philanthropic communities helped accelerate major gifts and pledges to the campaign.

According to Kenny, Alan Horwitz didn't make a leadership gift because he had the capacity to do so. He made a leadership gift because of the emotional connection he felt to the work PYB was doing in the community and to experiencing a similar life-altering event as one of the boys who participated in our program. It was this strong emotional connection, not simply his ability to give, which enabled PYB to secure his support. Beyond the obvious significance of a leadership gift of this magnitude, Kenny Holdsman points to the impact that a prominent gift can have on future donations. "A lead gift giver is a validator. Alan's presence as a supporter of our capital campaign had the important effect of lowering the risk for other potential major donors," said Kenny.

The reason for sharing this example is that giving at a high level isn't about what people can donate. It is about building a connection with them so that they will want to donate. Major donor support for a capital campaign, as PYB has shown us, is about relationships and relatability, not capacity. It's not about the marketing materials. It's about sharing a vision for how this campaign will transform lives and how a donor's support can be a catalyst for positive change.

Foundation Giving

Foundation giving is a very different animal than individual giving. Securing foundation support for your organization is predicated on a number of factors, and requires you to take a disciplined approach to researching opportunities, managing deadlines, and stewarding post-grant reporting.

Unlike individual donors who can be engaged and swayed on a more emotional level, institutional funders, like family and private foundations, make decisions differently. Institutional funders have stricter timeframes and processes to consider grant requests, and they also typically rely more heavily on measurement and evaluation data that demonstrates the impact of the potential grantee. Many foundations also have clear principles or areas of focus for the types of organizations they will and won't support.

The implications of these factors are as follows:

- **Alignment**: Nonprofits seeking grant support must conduct research to ensure that the mission and impact of the organization is in line with the giving principles of the funder. Regardless of how effective you may be as an arts organization, if the funder concentrates their grant dollars on environmental sustainability, or homelessness, or food insecurity, you would be wasting both your time and theirs if you submitted a request for support.

- **Measurement and evaluation**: To "win" amongst the numerous potential applicants, a nonprofit will likely need a strong evidence base showing that their organization's programming is having the desired impact on its target audience. It isn't enough (normally) to have a well-conceived mission or a few anecdotes from participants in your program. Based on various "Meet the Funders" panels I have attended over the years, many institutional funders will provide funding to between 5-10% of the organizations that apply for support. While there are many factors that funders consider when reaching their ultimate funding decision, in many cases what separates those who receive funding from those who do not is a clear demonstration of impact. We discuss measurement and evaluation in much more detail in Chapter 7.

- **Planning and cash flow**: Grant cycles can be long relative to some immediate short-term needs your agency may be facing. Even when the timelines between agency needs and potential grantor funding do line up, it is common for nonprofits to be rejected one or more times before being selected for funding. As a result, your grant planning has to anticipate a certain failure rate for submitted applications. Beyond that, agencies also have to plan for the fact that even successful submissions may not provide funds for a number of months down the road. Therefore, it is critical to carefully monitor and adjust your budget and cash flow projections when relying on grant funding.

Beyond these considerations, it is important to factor in the amount of time it takes to simply write and submit grant applications. While some sections of prior applications can be repurposed for future grants, strict adherence to word counts and other constraints requires that each submission be thoughtfully written.

Many nonprofits outsource grant writing, and there is no shortage of specialists that can be retained for this work. Best practices for bringing in a grant writer would include:

1. <u>Defining clear objectives</u>: Establish clear goals and expectations for the grant writer. This includes specifying which grants the consultant should target, the funding amounts needed, and any timing considerations. Clarity in these areas helps ensure alignment between your organization's needs and the consultant's efforts.

2. <u>Checking credentials and experience</u>: Look for consultants with a strong track record in grant writing, particularly in your nonprofit's sector and region. Experience with specific grantors or types of grants can be valuable information. If you are seeking government grants, then experience in this arena is critical to know upfront. Check references and ask for samples of successful grant proposals.

3. <u>Setting communication guidelines</u>: Decide how often you want updates and reports, and through what mediums (e.g., email updates, weekly calls). Regular communication helps keep an outside contractor on track and allows for timely adjustments.

4. <u>Providing necessary resources and access</u>: Ensure the consultant has access to all necessary documents and

information about your nonprofit. This includes background information, previous grant proposals, financial statements, and program impact data.

5. <u>Agreeing on a payment structure</u>: Determine if the payment will be hourly, per grant, or based on a monthly retainer.

6. <u>Outlining confidentiality parameters</u>: Specify that the information you're sharing must remain confidential before the consultant begins their work for your agency.

Regardless of whether you keep grant writing in-house or bring in a specialist to aid your efforts, remember that the grant writing process doesn't begin and end with a grant submission. Funder relationships can and should be cultivated. This helps establish an understanding of how your work and your potential funder are aligned. Whenever possible, try to establish some direct contact with a program officer or staff leader within the foundation before your grant is submitted. Invite funders to visit your place of business so that they can see your operation and gain a clearer picture of how you are making a difference. If you are fortunate enough to receive funding, closely adhere to whatever reporting guidelines they establish. The easiest way to not get a second grant is to not submit the necessary documentation from your first grant.

Corporate Giving

Chapter 4 of this book is dedicated to cultivating and retaining corporate partnerships. That said, it is important to address the role that corporate giving can have in your resource development plan, while also highlighting some of the challenges and limitations related to this aspect of fundraising.

As you may recall from the summary of the fundraising landscape provided above, corporate giving accounts for roughly 6% of charitable giving. Yet I can tell you from personal experience that board members in many situations dedicate a disproportionate amount of time and attention to the idea of attracting corporate resources.

It is important to acknowledge here that this type of giving is only a piece of the fundraising puzzle. Be aware of the potential risk of dedicating too much time and energy relative to the potential return. There is an expression "the juice isn't worth the squeeze". If you are only looking at what corporations can do for your organization financially, notwithstanding what other value those relationships can bring, then you may find that the effort required to attract these resources might be better spent in other types of fundraising. Beyond that, corporate giving typically involves a lot of restrictions from the donor for what may be a relatively small amount of dollars.

That is not to discourage you and your organization from pursuing corporate gifts. It is meant to caution you from relying too heavily on them vs other elements of a resource development plan.

Events

Many organizations build their development plan around a major fundraising event. This strategy can be a viable one. Events can be an effective way to focus your board, major donors, partners, and other stakeholders to support your organization. However, for any of us who have been involved with the planning and execution of a major fundraising event, we know how much work is involved to achieve the results we hope for.

There are numerous ways to structure an event, and there are a range of critical decisions that need to be made to help ensure its success. We will touch on a few of them here, but understand that this discussion only scratches the surface for event planning.

- **In person vs virtual**: Given the rapidly rising costs associated with venue rentals and catering, some nonprofits have shifted their events to being hybrid or even fully online. While this approach can greatly reduce costs, you also will lose the energy associated with having your community assembled together at one moment in time.

- **Ticket pricing**: Creating a tiered pricing structure, with higher prices associated with special experiences vs. general admission for the majority of attendees, can be a way to increase your proceeds from an event. On the other end of the spectrum, some agencies give certain target groups (students, young professionals, the elderly, etc.) reduced pricing to increase accessibility for that demographic group. The agency may also consider inviting guests at the organization's expense, allowing them to experience the magic of the organization first hand in the hopes of making a personal impact and securing financial support down the road. There are no right answers with pricing. It is important to consider different planning scenarios to see how alternative pricing models can impact your bottom line.

- **Sponsorship**: Attracting sponsor revenue can make or break the success of an event. I won't delve into how to price sponsorships, because so much of that is contextual for each event and prospective partner. What I will say is that you cannot get potential sponsors too early. Some major corporate sponsors plan their budgets up to a year in advance. As a result, make sure you are engaging potential sponsors no later than six months prior to your event, and even earlier if possible.

- **Budgeting**: In a recent event-planning webinar put on by the Chronicle of Philanthropy, it was suggested that you should budget for $1 in expense for every $3 you are hoping to raise at your event. While this is only a rule of thumb, it can give you an important benchmark when looking at where and how to spend your money. Areas that can be overlooked within the budget are the line items for lighting and audio/visual support. These items, while expensive, can help your event look and feel professionally run and help create the desired vibe of the evening.

In general, post-pandemic venue rentals and food & beverage prices have skyrocketed, so be sure to identify the current costs of these big line items early in your planning process. Also, know that vendor pricing can be negotiable and coordinated with sponsorship to lower your cost structure.

- **Revenue opportunities at your event**: We have all likely attended events with live and silent auctions. These auctions can provide important revenue for your agency, but donor fatigue related to auctions and the work associated with soliciting these items has caused auctions to decrease in their popularity.

  What is growing in popularity is the "paddle raise" style fundraising. This is where guests are encouraged to raise their paddle (or hand) at various price points to pledge a financial gift. Samantha Swaim, an event fundraising consultant, suggests that organizations have three different tiers of support during their paddle raise with those dollar figures tied to key milestones for the agency. For example, "We can send a child to camp for a week for $1,000. Who wants to help kids have a transformational experience by attending our camp?" Samantha's podcast, The Fundraising Elevator, covers the paddle raise and many other aspects and trends related to major fundraising events and I will point you toward this particular episode in the actionable next steps at the end of this chapter.

  There are numerous event fundraising platforms that can help facilitate paddle raise and auction components of your event. There is also the decision whether to hire someone to lead the live auction or paddle raise portion of your event. Again, there is no right answer as to whether this is the best use of your planning dollars. Only that you should weigh the pros and cons carefully when looking at how a celebrity or professional could impact your bottom line.

- **Leveraging your board**: Events can help galvanize your board to make their individual donations and also to engage their personal and professional networks. Having ticket sale goals for each board member or a pricing structure that incentivizes them to purchase a table (or two) is a common and effective practice. Board members need to not only show up for your event, but also take a leading role in helping to guarantee its success.

- **Honored guests and hosts committees**: Integrating a host committee and having special honorees can be an effective mechanism to recruit influential volunteers to play a leading role in your event. Honored guests can (and should) help recruit attendees and the organization can help recognize the important contributions they have made to your mission. Host committees can be a catalyst for ticket sales, motivating members of your community to take an active role in promoting the event. These structures (and others) have the potential to pay huge dividends, but they all require careful planning.

- **In-house led vs consultant-led events**: Many agencies lean into consultant support to help them navigate many of the above issues with event planning and execution. That said, the cost to engage a consultant vs leading these efforts internally can be a major investment. It is also vital for leaner organizations to be self-aware about how much major event planning and implementation could shift the focus of manpower away from doing the mission-critical work of the organization. Events are a major drain of time and talent. Make sure this aspect of event planning is given proper consideration by staff and board leadership when contemplating embedding a major event in your calendar.

Earned Income

Many nonprofit organizations benefit from earned income, which can help diversify their funding sources beyond traditional donations and grants. The types of earned income that your organization might be able to access will differ based on circumstances that are particular to each entity such as the sector your work is involved with, whether you have physical space or not and other variables. Here are some common types of earned income that nonprofits can take advantage of:

1. <u>Fee-for-service</u>: This includes income derived from the services provided by the nonprofit to its clients or the public. Examples include tuition for educational programs, fees for counseling services, or charges for healthcare services.

2. <u>Membership fees</u>: Nonprofits that operate on a membership model can collect dues or fees from individuals or organizations that wish to join. These fees often come with benefits, such as access to exclusive resources, events, or networking opportunities.

3. <u>Product sales</u>: Some nonprofits generate income by selling products related to their mission. For example, a nonprofit focused on employment training might sell products made by program participants, or a wildlife conservation group might sell educational materials or eco-friendly merchandise. Many organizations sell branded merchandise to increase both revenue and visibility for their agency.

4. <u>Conferences and events</u>: Hosting events, such as conferences, workshops, or seminars, can generate income through ticket sales, registration fees, and sometimes sponsorships. These events often also serve as educational or promotional opportunities for the nonprofit and can elevate their status as a thought leader on a topic related to their mission.

5. <u>Facility rentals</u>: Nonprofits that own property can earn income by renting out space for events, meetings, or other functions. This can include renting a hall for a special occasion or subleasing office space to other organizations.

If earned income is part of your development strategy, consult your tax professional to understand whether these and any other forms of earned income are classified as "unrelated" income, which would then require your nonprofit organization to pay taxes on this revenue.

Bequests

Bequests or planned gifts are where an individual would identify a financial gift or other assets to be made to a nonprofit organization after they pass away. The CCS Fundraising Landscape report cited earlier in this chapter estimates that about 9% of charitable donations come from planned gifts. While this philanthropic amount is quite significant in aggregate, nonprofit organizations should know that this form of charitable giving is complex and requires legal and financial planning support that is normally outside of what most small to mid-sized agencies would have access to. That does not mean that your organization shouldn't begin to have these kinds of conversations with select individual major donors. Organizations should also recognize, however, that revenue from these types of gifts is not something that can be earmarked in any particular year and requires a different level of planning and support than typical major gifts solicitations entail.

Give/Get Policy for Your Board

For many organizations, the Board of Directors is a key element of their fundraising effort. Many organizations still maintain a give/get policy with board members, whereby each member is expected to either donate a certain amount of money annually (give) or engage their personal and professional networks to attract financial resources (get). As discussed in the Board Development chapter of this book (Chapter 2), the conversation about a board member's role in fundraising cannot start after they are voted into the organization. Fundraising in general, and annual goals in particular, should be articulated to prospective board members in the recruiting and vetting process.

In my early days as an Executive Director, I was so thankful that people had agreed to support Pitch In for Baseball and Softball as board members that I didn't want to push the topic of money very hard. The board had a lot of passion and energy and it was easy to be thankful for what they were doing, and subsequently not acknowledge what they weren't doing. Not everyone is comfortable even talking about the subject of money. Our implicit biases and hesitations about the topic can often rise to the forefront when we try to approach the topic of money with our board. However, by not having these conversations we can also risk the very viability of the nonprofit we are trying to build.

Many startup organizations fall into this trap. We invite our friends and family to be part of the founding board, and then when the business of supporting the organization comes around, things can get challenging or awkward. We don't want to damage the relationships we have with people we care about, so while we encourage people to give, we never set clear expectations for how much giving is needed.

The entire notion of a give/get target is a subject of great debate. As organizations seek to increase the racial, ethnic, and age diversity of their boards, there is an acknowledgment that give/get targets can create a burden or unreasonable expectation for people who are in very different places in their career journeys, have had very different lived experiences, or who don't have access to the same type of resources or professional networks.

One solution to the firm give/get approach is a framework that I adopted early at Pitch In for Baseball and Softball that has had increasing popularity in recent years. Instead of setting a specific number as the fundraising goal of each board member, we asked them to make a gift that was "personally meaningful to them." Based on their own personal financial position and their other charitable giving, a gift of $100 may be significant for some of your board members. If that is the case, then they would have met an important standard of board engagement by making a gift of that amount. For other individuals, a gift of $10,000 may actually not be deeply meaningful to them even though it may meet or exceed the target set by the organization.

Establishing a give/get target or not or whether to have a framework that is more nuanced is complex and requires ongoing discussion between staff leadership and the board. There is no one size fits all solution to this topic. Regardless of where your organization lands on this issue, staff leadership can create a resource development plan with each board member that is tailored and appropriate for them.

Making a gift is not the only way a board member can support the organization or be engaged in resource development. As discussed previously, board members can (and should) play a major role in identifying, cultivating, recruiting, and stewarding potential donors. They can host events in their homes or places of business. Board members can introduce us to potential corporate partners or institutional funders. They can help us obtain in-kind donations. They can help us gain access to technical or functional support within their respective companies. As an example, corporations may have website design, video production, legal, accounting, or social media expertise that can be extremely valuable to a nonprofit organization. By taking a more holistic approach to resource development, each board member can make a meaningful contribution to the organization, which can extend well beyond their topline revenue figure.

The Role of Your Board in Identifying Prospects

Beyond the give/get policy your organization establishes and in addition to whatever gift that member makes personally, a fundamental expectation for most board members is to be someone who "opens doors" for the organization. Board members who care deeply about the mission of the agency should want to see it grow. One of the ways to help it grow is to bring new prospects closer to the organization. Those prospects could be individuals, corporations, foundations, or entities who could make gifts-in-kind. It is important to clarify to the board member that they don't have to be the person making the final ask for the gift or solidifying the corporate partnership. Their role in this process is to introduce the lead fundraiser at the organization to the prospect and to convey that they as a board member are deeply committed to the future success of the nonprofit. If they want to stay involved in the cultivation beyond that point, that's great. If they don't have the time or inclination to be involved beyond that introduction, that is also great. What they need to do is help make a "warm" introduction to the staff leadership so that they can cultivate this new relationship.

Summary

Resource development is as vital to your organization's sustainability as anything you will do. It requires planning, determination, and a collaborative approach between board and staff to increase your likelihood of achieving your fundraising goals. There are rarely quick fixes or easy answers. Donor cultivation, conversion, and stewardship involve coordination and clear communication. It can be done and it has to be done.

Actionable Next Steps

1. Analyze your donor data from the last three years and create a donor revenue pie for your organization. How does it compare to the national averages and does this point to opportunities for your organization?

2. Identify your top 15 individual donors and schedule time in the next three months to talk with them in person (and thank them). If you aren't sure how to structure these meetings, scan this QR code to grab some free time on my calendar and I can provide some guidance.

3. Scan this QR code to listen to Samantha Swaim's January 24, 2024 Fundraising Elevator podcast where she discusses how to construct and leverage a paddle raise for your next event.

4. Put the topic of your organization's give/get on the agenda for your next board meeting. How do your members feel about it and should you consider a different approach?

5. Ask each current board member to identify two prospects that they are willing to connect the staff leadership to within the next 60 days.

CHAPTER 4:
Building Your Partnership Portfolio

Chapter Overview: This chapter delves into how to identify potential corporate partners, strategies to get the critical first meeting, and what to do (and not do) when you do get in front of prospective partners.

Have you ever had a board member suggest that you contact a professional sports franchise or a major corporation for partnership with your nonprofit agency? It happened to me frequently. I'm sure many of you have had similar "helpful" ideas from your board without any suggestion of how you are supposed to accomplish this.

Partnership development was the single most critical element of our growth strategy at Pitch In for Baseball and Softball (PIFBS). It fueled our revenue engine. It wildly expanded our social media reach and impact. And it was loads of fun!

What hasn't been shared yet is how much time, effort and worry it took to build these partnerships. Was it worth it? Yes! Was it easy? Hell no!!

What is (and isn't) a Partnership

Before we move ahead with how you might create a robust and successful partnership development strategy, let's set the landscape for what is a partnership and what isn't a partnership.

Having a corporation or a team donate something to your annual gala, or even becoming a title sponsor, is not partnering. These are transactions. Company A writes your organization a check for a certain amount and in exchange they receive certain things…tickets, placement in a program, etc. In most of these cases, the nonprofit organization is extracting a majority of the value from this relationship while the company is simply fulfilling its obligation as a corporate entity within the community.

A partnership is different. It's not transactional. Done right, it can be transformational for the nonprofit and deeply meaningful for the corporation. In a true partnership, each party derives meaningful benefit from the relationship. In a partnership, each side is excited about working with the other and both parties are curious about how the relationship might grow in the future.

An Entitlement Mindset

So how do you go about cultivating and nurturing win/win partnerships? It starts with your mindset. Many organizations take what can be characterized as an "entitlement mindset" to partnership development. Spoiler alert, this is not the way to go. An entitlement mindset is indicative of an organization that thinks or acts in the following ways:

- What can the partner do for us?

- They should definitely want to help us given our mission.

- I'm sure _____ celebrity or large corporation will want to become involved with us given our work with children.

- Let's just call them. They will help us.

- Look how much they spend on _____. I can't believe they won't be able to write us a check for $100,000.

Many of us have had these thoughts. It's human nature to a great extent. But these thoughts and questions are focused on what the partner can do for you and forget the critical element of looking at the relationship from their perspective. If you let an entitlement mindset permeate your partnership development efforts, you are doomed from the start.

A Value-Oriented Mindset

So what is the right approach or mindset? It starts with the perspective of making sure your organization brings real value to the partnership. Having a value-oriented mindset will force you to invest significant time and effort before ever making an attempt to contact a prospective partner.

You want to ask yourself (and then answer) some of the following questions:

- Why would they choose us over another nonprofit in the same space?

- What employee engagement opportunities/social media content/audiences can we provide to the partner that they can't access or create on their own?

- How can we make this partnership transformational and sustainable rather than transactional?

Doing Your Homework

Partnership development is a bit like an iceberg. While the public can see the 10% of the iceberg that is above the surface, the real meat of partnership development happens below the surface and out of the view of the public. What happens behind the scenes ensures you are prepared and ready to engage a potential partner. In my mind, preparation to prospect for potential partners involves three primary areas:

- **Values:** Focusing on the alignment between what a potential partner cares about and how it aligns with the work your organization does.

- **Connections:** Searching for linkages to prospective partner organizations that can foster a warm introduction.

- **Emotions:** Curating internal assets, like pictures or impact stories, that you can share with partners so that they can form a strong emotional connection to your organization.

Shared Values

The foundation of any long-term partnership is a strong alignment between the giving focus of the prospective partner and the impact your organization has on its target population. For example, if your arts or youth sports or environmental sustainability organization is considering approaching a bank that focuses its charitable giving on increasing financial literacy, you'll soon realize there is very little your organization can do to align with them in any sort of meaningful strategic partnership.

That said, it does not mean you can't highlight a specific aspect of your programmatic work when approaching a partner. In the case of Pitch In for Baseball and Softball, many of our corporate partners had focus areas that weren't specific to baseball or softball. They might have focused on youth development or disaster relief or supporting under-resourced communities. By repositioning or broadening your agency's definition of who you serve and the impact you are making, you can in turn broaden your list of potential partners.

Finding a Connection

Identifying strategic alignment between the prospective partner and your organization is only step one in the process. Once that strategic fit is validated, the next step is finding a way in the door. While there may be a temptation to reach out directly to the prospect and seek the opportunity to connect, this approach will likely not yield a positive outcome. Reaching out to someone you don't know and who doesn't know you is what the sales industry would refer to as "cold calling." In contrast, if someone that the target prospect knows and trusts makes the introduction on your behalf, your chances of success go up significantly. Experience shows that you are at least ten times more likely to get a meeting with a "warm introduction" than without one and I'm probably understating that number.

So who should reach out to broker this warm introduction? The answer is whoever you know best, regardless of their title or role. The general rule of thumb is the more senior the contact the better, but that doesn't inherently mean someone high up in corporate giving. If they are in a powerful enough position and can vouch for you and/or the organization, then you are more than halfway to getting a face to face meeting with a prospect.

This is where you can lean on resources like LinkedIn and your board to uncover relationships. Ultimately, all you are really looking for is an inside "champion" or friend to make an email introduction between you and the decision makers within the organization. Once that happens, you at least have a fighting chance for engaging in serious partnership conversations. (We will talk more about what to do in that first partnership cultivation meeting a little bit later in this chapter.)

In other cases, it's simply being in the right place at the right time. A perfect example tracing back to PIFBS was when I happened to run into the VP of Human Resources for a Major League Baseball team on a bus heading from the airport to an industry meeting. We struck up a conversation on the 15-minute ride, and I was able to leverage that connection into an email introduction to the team's Community Affairs and Partnership Development divisions. While it took over 18 months to figure out how our organizations would work together, the resulting relationship was well worth the time and energy. You never know when opportunity will knock and that is why it is so important for you and other members of your agency to always wear your partnership development hat.

Curating Shareable Assets

While you are building your prospect pipeline and seeking your inside contacts who can open the door, you also need to make sure that you have fully armed yourself with all of the impact data, stories, quotes, pictures, and videos that you can. Every partnership pitch needs to be customized. You can't expect to present the same PowerPoint deck and have the same conversation with each prospect. While it sounds a bit tedious, the key to this is not only finding the right images and stories that your agency has amassed over the years, but labeling and organizing the files in such a manner that enables you to search and find them easily. Having all of these assets at your digital fingertips will be valuable as you seek to personalize your pitch and make sure it lands with the right emotion and impact when you get in front of your potential partner.

DOs and DON'Ts of Your First Prospect Meeting

To quote my old friends at Head and Shoulders, "You never get a second chance to make a first impression," and you won't get a second meeting with a prospective partner if you don't nail the first meeting. So how can you increase your chances of success in the first meeting?

The first thing you need to do is think about the meeting from the perspective of your audience. They expect you to come in with a compelling story about how important your work is as a way to then ask for money to help solve your problems. The quickest way to shut down the possibility of a new relationship is to lunge for their corporate wallet. In fact, I like to think about the image of the prospect with their hands stuffed in their pockets protecting their wallet to reinforce the idea of being patient about asking for money.

Instead, what I have found is that the first meeting is an important opportunity to show the prospect that you are a sophisticated and mature organization, and that you as the leader of that organization can be trusted as a potential partner. On a more fundamental level, you are hoping to get them to like you and see real value in the possibility of working together. With that in mind, I like to structure the meeting around getting the partner to do a lot of the talking. Of course I'm prepared to discuss my entity and our programs, but I want to learn more about what they think and how they make funding decisions.

I used to feel like I needed to come in with all the answers and the perfect partnership proposal in the initial face-to-face meeting. What I evolved to understand is that I was putting all the pressure on me to hit a target when I didn't really even know what all the rules of the game were. Wouldn't it be easier to customize a partnership approach if you had deeper insight into what the partner valued, and what their typical budget range is for new partners?

Armed with this approach, I suggest an initial meeting focused around gaining answers to questions such as these:

1. *What was it about our organization that resonated enough with you that you agreed to spend time with us today?*

   By asking a question like this, you are hoping to uncover what emotional chord your organization struck with them. Are they just kicking the tires on your organization, or is there some kind of deeper connection that you can build off of in the future?

2. *Are you hoping to engage your employees in a potential partnership?*

   This is a very nonthreatening question and should be easy to address. Many companies are actively seeking ways for their employees to engage with their nonprofit partners. Knowing that is the case, you may want to be prepared to discuss how your team engages the employees of another partner to let them know this is something you are both willing to do and experienced in doing successfully.

3. *Are you open to talking about a potential partnership on social media?*

   I like to incorporate this question so that I can begin to understand if there are ways to add value from the partnership beyond the idea of them simply writing a check. In seeking social media support with a partner, you are asking for something that doesn't affect their charitable giving budget. Some corporate partners have massive audiences. Some potential partners have dedicated social media and video content creators who could be allocated to enhance the partnership. In multiple situations where Pitch In for Baseball and Softball worked with Major League teams, their willingness and ability to create and share video content more than doubled the value of those partnerships.

4. *Can you give an example of an existing partnership that you would describe as very successful and what factors led to that success?*

   In this question, I am looking for certain qualities or characteristics of the relationship that I could incorporate into a future partnership discussion with this audience. For example, if the prospect describes the key aspect of one of their successful existing relationships is that the nonprofit's event activation is "turnkey," then I would be sure to include the word turnkey in any future proposal with them. Likewise, if they described the importance of how the nonprofit shared critical impact data, then I would be mindful to underscore how other partners were given access to impact data to enhance their content that they might share internally or externally. Again, you are looking for clues (or in some cases, flashing neon signs) that say what this partner values, and you want to emphasize these elements in any proposal you might share in the future.

5. *For organizations that you do support financially, what is a typical range?*

   Ok, we went four questions without bringing up money, but we also don't want to leave this meeting without more perspective on this topic. Framing the question in this manner isn't threatening or presumptuous. It is mature and thoughtful, gives them some latitude to respond, and could ultimately provide you with an invaluable piece of data as you consider how to launch this particular partnership.

6. My last question is *would it be ok if I followed up with you in two to three weeks regarding how we might work together?*

Partnerships are not a one-call-close type of sales environment. If your target company is large enough, many people might ultimately need to be involved in a go/no go decision. By asking for additional time, you are letting them know you are being thoughtful about the relationship and that you are seeking to customize your proposal based on the information you obtained in the first meeting. This will also give the prospect time to gain some internal alignment and potentially bring other stakeholders and decision makers into the critical second conversation.

Meet Joe Waters

The best and clearest voice on the topic of corporate partnerships for me is Joe Waters. Behind his wicked Boston accent is a person who has been immersed in partnership development and cause marketing throughout the majority of his career. Joe's initial success as the Director of Cause and Event Marketing at Boston Medical Center was the springboard for him to be a national thought-leader on partnership marketing.

Joe looks at corporate partnerships like an ice cream sundae. In his view, partnerships are the cherry on top of your organization. They aren't something you create. They are the result of everything you've done. If your programs are strong, and your evidence base is clear, and your branding is well defined, and your target audience sees value in your work, and your board is engaged in your capacity building, then you can win in the world of corporate partnerships. Partnerships are a means to build off your success, not a quick fix when other things aren't going right.

Joe preaches that companies look for audiences to tell them what is good, popular, and profitable in this world. So what that means is that companies are looking for organizations that have strong audiences, which also means they have a strong brand because of that audience's positive perception. When organizations do a good job cultivating and growing a strong brand and community, that's ultimately what leads to corporate partnership success. We talk extensively about brand building and your communications strategies in Chapters 8 & 9.

Charity Partnerships vs Marketing Partnerships

Joe draws a critical distinction between a charitable partnership and one that is rooted in marketing. In this paradigm, charity partnerships are when a company supports you because they just love what you do. It's an extension of individual giving. Maybe you have a great donor who has supported your organization, someone who just happens to run 20 convenience stores, and one day they say, "Hey, I want to do this program for you in my store." This is a classic example of a typical charity partnership.

But where Joe sees the sector heading is more in the direction of marketing partnerships. In these relationships, a company says hey, I see a bottom line benefit to working with your organization. Now I may also have a very strong positive feeling about your organization, but I also see an opportunity with your organization to help me achieve my corporate goals of increasing my customer base, increasing brand awareness, making my employees happy, etc.

In this aspect of partnership development, Joe emphasizes to his nonprofit clients the importance of building their audience… an audience that knows, likes and trusts you, one that you have the ability to influence. That audience must exist somewhere, whether that be on an email distribution list, a community on Instagram, or subscribers to a YouTube channel.

Joe highlighted the example of the marketing partnership between the National Audubon Society and Allbirds, the makers of sustainable shoes and clothing. The National Audubon Society had a social media audience of over a million followers. Allbirds proposed making a line of shoes specifically for their audience. The Audubon Society promoted the opportunity. Allbirds sold the shoes, while the Audubon Society was able to achieve some meaningful proceeds from the program.

A Partnership Cultivation Framework

Joe's framework for partnership cultivation is grounded in what he calls prospecting circles. There are three levels to prospecting circles: the inner circle is the bullseye, followed next by the prospect, and then the suspect on the outside. Joe tells people to focus on the bullseye first…the people who know, like, and trust you. In reality, it seems that most nonprofits do the opposite. They start on the outside with some high-profile targets who don't know the nonprofit, and who the nonprofit has no real connection to. All that leads to is wasted time and effort.

When Joe started at Boston Medical Center, he had zero corporate partners. He did, however, have a few passionate donors, including a gentleman who owned a discount retailer called Ocean State Job Lots. Joe approached the owner about doing something in his stores and lo and behold he raised over $450,000 in three weeks. Joe then did what he described as leapfrogging. He took that successful experience and used it to land his next partner and so on and so on. Ultimately, he used his successful case studies and their referrals to build a network of 40 corporate partners. It all started with someone in his bullseye who knew, liked, and trusted him and the nonprofit.

When launching a prospecting initiative, many organizations start by asking their board who they know or who they can introduce them to. Many times they will say they don't know anyone. If that is truly the case, then they might be the wrong board member. Beyond board connections, organizations may find valuable opportunities right in front of them with current vendors or current donors. Remember, those donors likely work for some company, or in some cases might own their own company, that could fit the bill of a valuable potential partner. Joe pointed to the Boston Food Bank as an example of leaning into existing donors to gain access to partnership opportunities. The food bank hired someone in the partnership development team and intentionally paired them with a major gifts officer so that they could try to leverage those existing donor relationships into warm introductions which could potentially lead to corporate partnerships. While this approach seems logical, many organizations have major donor officers and partnership development teams in separate silos and don't take advantage of this opportunity.

One other approach that Joe utilizes is trying to identify event sponsors and reimagine their connection into larger and less transactional relationships. Sponsorship is just one of a number of ways a company can support a nonprofit. There is employee engagement, cause marketing, influencer marketing, C-suite giving, and employee giving just to name a few. Joe cited the example of a local grocery store that decides to be a $5,000 supporter of a nonprofit's annual gala. Instead of letting that be the end of their relationship, however, the nonprofit could reach out to the store and expand their work together by exploring how to engage shoppers in raising $25,000. In the end, Joe feels that corporate partnerships are too hard to create to only do one thing with them. Just because a relationship starts in one place does not mean it has to stay there.

In another example, Joe described a board member who lived next to the owner of a chain of 348 convenience stores, but didn't think of them when asked to identify prospects for the organization. Our networks are much larger than our professional connections. You just have to keep your partnership hat on all the time, and keep mining your board, donors, volunteers, and staff for information about who they know. The bottom line is, they probably know more people than they initially might think.

One simple trick I use is to always look at the email address of donors. If the donor's email was something @staples.com or @goldmansachs.com, then I'd try to find out what they did at those companies and if they might be willing to help us with an introduction to a key decision maker.

Summary

The beauty of partnership marketing is that every nonprofit can play in this arena regardless of their size. If you have a definable, meaningful audience and a clear brand, then you have some of the fundamentals in place to pursue partnerships. When you do consider partnerships, look at the value you can add to them and not just what they can do for you. As you look for potential partners, look at those individuals and relationships where someone who already knows, likes, and trusts you can make a warm introduction for you. Then when you get into a first meeting, become an active listener. Use what you learn to customize a proposal that meets the needs of both sides. Partnerships can add so much to your organization. It's really about getting those first one or two partners on board any way you can and building out from there.

Actionable Next Steps

1. Examine how your agency is labeling and storing important pictures. Create a clear and consistent system so you can search and access these easily in the future.

2. Scan this QR code to subscribe to Joe Waters' newsletter at Selfish Giving.

3. Put the topic of partnership development on the agenda for your next board meeting for discussion.

4. Block out one hour per week on your calendar for the next month to do research on prospective partners to see if their giving focus aligns with your organization's impact or target audience.

CHAPTER 5:
Building Your Financial Controls

Chapter Overview: *This chapter outlines the importance of having strong financial controls and transparent conversations between the board and staff leadership regarding the financial health of your organization. In addition, this chapter highlights the need to closely monitor cash flow.*

As the CEO of a nonprofit, understanding the organization's finances is not a box that you simply check and move on. It's a process that should never end. While you may not have academic training or past experience in preparing and managing budgets, you will now be looked upon to do so. Since you can't run from the issue of understanding your budget and creating financial oversight, you might as well embrace it.

Assessing the Organization's Financial Health

If you are entering an organization as its Executive Director, I cannot think of a higher priority than understanding its financial condition. One simple and practical piece of advice is having a weekly meeting with your finance team, whatever that might mean for your entity. That may be a weekly/monthly call with your board's treasurer or your CFO. You may also need a regular meeting with your development team to maintain a clear understanding of how topline revenue is trending.

An important element of these budget or resource development conversations is to develop a culture of transparency. These are opportunities to openly discuss the mission-critical financial aspects of the organization without judgment or assessing blame. Let them know that your questions are simply a vehicle to bring you up to speed and enable you to plan more effectively. Encourage all members of your team to not run from bad news. The sooner challenges can be brought into the light of day, the sooner that creative minds can develop solutions to address these challenges.

In terms of the resource development side of the business, one valuable approach is to assess a likelihood of bringing in each desired gift, grant, or sponsorship based on the history and current state of each of those relationships. You can even assign a probability to each major development line item to give your budget some scenarios in terms of likely vs optimistic outcomes.

As part of this deep dive into revenue projection and monitoring, a best practice is to engage each of these donors throughout the year and not just when you are anticipating making the ask. In the case where you might be a new Executive Director, your arrival into the organization creates a logical opportunity with these donors to sit down and understand their mindset and priorities.

How do they feel about the organization?

- What is it about your organization that has led them to become a supporter?

- Would they be open to multi-year commitments/pledges to your organization to facilitate your ability to develop long term strategic plans?

- When was the last time they met with the constituents you are trying to serve? Are there moments in the coming months when it might make the most sense for them to attend or participate?

- Are there any changes coming in terms of the giving priorities of this funder? If so, will those changes likely benefit your organization or put its funding in jeopardy?

- Are there ideas or opportunities that they would like to see the organization pursue? If there are, this might create an opportunity for you to go back to this funder if this opportunity becomes part of your future plans.

Regardless of the exact questions you ask, go in with a listening mindset. Start each of the conversations by thanking the funder for their past support and highlight the impact that their prior gifts have made on the communities you are trying to support.

Don't use the meeting as a chance to impress the funder or sell them on your approach to leading the organization. That doesn't mean you shouldn't prepare a concise elevator pitch on your experience and priorities, but prepare to listen more than you talk.

Typical Financial Statements

Having run a for-profit business for 12 years before entering the nonprofit sector and possessing an MBA from The Wharton School, I had a good working knowledge of how to interpret financial statements. That being said, not all Executive Directors or board members have a strong financial background.

As part of the normal course of understanding how your organization is doing from an economic perspective and in keeping your Board of Directors informed on these matters, most nonprofit organizations produce four different types of financial statements.

1. <u>Statement of financial position (balance sheet)</u>: This statement provides a snapshot of the organization's financial condition at a specific point in time. It lists the nonprofit's assets (what it owns), liabilities (what it owes), and net assets (the difference between assets and liabilities, similar to equity in for-profit businesses).

2. <u>Statement of activities (income statement)</u>: This statement shows the organization's revenues and expenses over a period of time. It helps stakeholders understand how the organization is funded and how those funds are being spent. It may also be segmented to show changes in unrestricted, temporarily restricted, and permanently restricted net assets.

3. <u>Statement of functional expenses:</u> This statement categorizes expenses according to purpose. Expenses are broken down into program services (costs related to the mission of the nonprofit) and supporting services (management, general administration, and fundraising costs). This breakdown of what percentage of expenses go directly to programs vs "overhead" is a benchmark some funders will look at when considering the efficiency of an organization.

4. <u>Statement of cash flows:</u> This statement provides a summary of the cash inflows and outflows over a period of time, segmented into operating, investing, and financing activities. These sections help show how the organization manages its cash resources.

   a. **Operating activities.** These activities refer to the revenue and expenses associated with operating your nonprofit. Staff salaries, program fees, and donations are included in this section.

   b. **Investing activities.** In your statement of cash flows, you'll list information such as long-term investment purchases and sales, including property and equipment. Interest earned on your investments would also be included.

   c. **Financing activities.** Finance activities include the issuance and repayment of equity, issuance and repayment of debt, and capital lease obligations.

If your agency uses accounting software, like QuickBooks, then these reports can be generated automatically. All you need to do is select the report and the date (or date range) you want the report to include. These reports can be utilized by your treasurer, finance committee, or whoever is primarily responsible for financial oversight to keep abreast of the financial state of the entity and provide perspective for staff leadership and the full board.

Monitoring Cash Flow

In developing your deep understanding of the financial health of the organization, it is vital to keep a keen eye on cash flow in particular. Just because your nonprofit is on track to meet its overall budget, doesn't mean that cash flow will be available to meet payroll, rent, or whatever ongoing fixed or variable expenses you may have.

Unlike many for-profit businesses which have revenue that can in many ways be described as smooth, nonprofit organizations are mostly characterized by revenue which could be best described as uneven or sporadic. Major individual gifts might come in close to the end of the calendar year. Revenue from grants and events may come in as large lump sums in many cases. Government contracts may come in well after services are rendered. For these and other reasons, understanding and anticipating cash flow challenges can enable you to work with funders to potentially smooth out your cash flow. Likewise, you could encourage board members to accelerate their annual contributions so that they don't fall right at the end of the calendar year.

Despite efforts to avoid cash flow shortfalls, sometimes they cannot be avoided. However if you can accurately forecast these challenges you can work with your bank or other financial institutions to develop a line of credit to give your organization the liquidity it needs to handle day to day expenses until revenue comes in to put the organization back on track. I recommend creating a cash flow budget which shows anticipated cash reserves at the end of each month based on anticipated revenues and projected expenses. If a challenging portion of the year is expected, then you will have time to make plans in advance instead of going into emergency response mode.

Financial Controls

We have all seen the unfortunate stories where a member of a nonprofit organization has embezzled funds and potentially puts the future of that organization at risk. Financial controls might vary significantly given the size and complexity of your operation. But the size of the organization does not excuse the lack of reasonable financial controls. Here are some examples of financial controls that could ensure that the funds your organization has worked so hard to secure can be used for their intended purpose:

1. <u>Segregation of duties</u>: Divide responsibilities among different individuals to reduce the risk of error or fraud. For example, the person who authorizes transactions should not be the same person who records them.

2. <u>Bank reconciliations</u>: Perform monthly bank reconciliations to ensure that the cash balances in your internal books match the bank statements, identifying and investigating any discrepancies.

3. Approval authority: Establish clear authority limits for approving expenditures and contracts. Larger transactions should require higher-level approval.

4. Cash handling controls: Implement controls over cash receipts and disbursements, including secure storage, deposit procedures, and use of official receipts.

5. Procurement policies: Develop and enforce policies for procurement to ensure fair and transparent purchasing processes and to prevent conflicts of interest.

6. Grant management: For nonprofits that receive grants, maintain strict control over grant funds, ensuring that they are used in accordance with donor restrictions and reporting requirements.

7. Investment policy: If your nonprofit has investable assets, adopt an investment policy that outlines the objectives, risk tolerance, and allocation strategies approved by the Board of Directors.

8. Document retention policy: Implement a policy for retaining financial records and documents for the period required by law, ensuring their availability for audit and review.

9. Training and education: Provide regular training for staff and board members on financial policies, procedures, and best practices to ensure compliance and understanding.

10. Cybersecurity measures: Protect financial information through robust cybersecurity measures, including secure networks, password policies, and regular backups.

Engaging Your Board in Financial Oversight

Fiduciary responsibility is one of the most fundamental responsibilities of the Board of Directors. At a minimum, this would include approving the agency's Form 990 as well as the financial statements and annual budget. Your board might/should have a finance committee that helps facilitate these processes, reviews, and reporting.

That being said, not every board takes an active interest in the financial oversight of the organization. In my experience, there was general apathy toward the budget. Many board members are deeply interested in programs and strategy, but that same enthusiasm doesn't extend to the less sexy aspect of board service such as financial management. The Pitch In for Baseball and Softball Board trusted me to manage the finances. That said, there was one board member who could be counted on to ask a few pertinent questions. His questions were always fair and relatively easy to address which then led to the approval of the budget and the acceptance of the annual financial statements and Form 990. While not having a robust debate over the budget might make for an efficient board meeting, it is not always in the best interest of the organization.

One way to facilitate conversation is to prepare and share the budget well in advance of the board meeting where it will be considered. Send out an executive summary of the budget and highlight key areas where there are differences from prior years and where the organization has the most risk. These risks might center around the revenue side of the equation due to the nature of your donors. Conversely, they could be focused more on the expense side if you are launching or expanding particular programs or if you have supplies that may be exposed to supply chain or inflationary influences. Regardless of the circumstances, the communication in advance of that board meeting should set the expectation that board members come prepared with questions. Let them know that open conversation is important and needed so that the organization moves forward with a budget that reflects the best thinking of its leadership. Wherever possible, the budget should have contingencies if specific revenue or expense items fall outside of what is expected.

Hire a CFO

Depending on the size of the organization and its operating budget, it may not be feasible to actually hire someone whose job it is to manage the finances of the organization. In many lean organizations, the job of developing and managing the budget falls squarely onto the shoulders of the Executive Director. If this is the case, then the next best scenario would be to look to the board for support in understanding and reporting on the financial health of the organization. If that experience doesn't currently exist on the board, then work closely with the Board President to make this skill set a priority for inclusion on the board moving forward.

Summary

Understanding and being in command of the financial state of the organization may not be what drives your passion, but it is a vital part of nonprofit management. Properly stewarding the funds that come into your nonprofit is a fundamental responsibility. If you have this experience in your toolkit, use it to help bring other team members up to your level of financial fluency. If not, seek out resources and develop financial controls to give you the perspective and confidence you need to address financial matters. Don't run from financial challenges or look to assign blame. Create a culture of transparency and engage your staff and board to help strengthen the financial foundation of your organization.

Actionable Next Steps

1. Schedule a recurring meeting with your key financial officer, whoever that may be within your entity. These should occur at least once a month.

2. Review the list of financial controls listed above. See which one or two of these controls makes the most sense for your organization to incorporate first and then go on from there.

3. Make cash flow and your agency's cash position a regular topic at board meetings. Too often boards focus on the budget and not on cash flow.

4. If you are fortunate enough to have a cash reserve, call your bank to look at safe investment opportunities.

CHAPTER 6:
Building Your Programs

Chapter Overview: *This chapter discusses the challenges and considerations related to program adaptation and growth. It also provides guidance for understanding the true costs of your programs.*

Your programs are the lifeblood of your organization in many respects. Your programs are how you accomplish your mission. They are how you interact with your community. All of the fundraising, volunteer engagement, board development, and staff hiring we conduct is done so that we can offer programs that positively impact the constituents we serve.

Program Growth

Jackie Einstein Astrof is the passionate founder and now Board Chair for PennPAC. PennPAC mobilizes teams of University of Pennsylvania alumni to strengthen nonprofits through their pro bono consulting services. According to Jackie, "One of the best decisions I made in regards to the long term success of the organization was focusing on quality and not quantity when it came to our programs. Maybe it's the benefit of not having shareholders to answer to or the pressure to sell more widgets that enabled us to take this approach. We wanted to make sure that there was integrity in the consulting experience both for our nonprofit clients and for our volunteers."

The PennPAC "quality over quantity" approach isn't adhered to universally. Many organizations can get out over their skis and try to expand the reach or scope of their programs too quickly, or attempt to expand too far geographically before they are ready. Adding wraparound services can be the other side of the coin of mission creep. Scale is a buzzword heard all too often in the boardrooms of nonprofit organizations. The eagerness to serve more people in need comes from a good place in most instances. However, organizations can fail to properly anticipate if they have the resources and infrastructure available to replicate their initial successes at a larger scale. Yes, growth is important in any business, but at what rate? Do we have the discipline to know when too much is not the right thing?

Managing Change

Jeff Breslin is the Executive Director of the Boys and Girls Clubs of Baltimore. His experience provides some critical perspective when looking at how to manage program changes and growth. Jeff reflected on the principles that helped his organization survive and thrive through the pandemic, which came down to consistency and persistence. "Once we realized that we could stay open safely, we communicated that we would be open on these days, and during these hours, and then we were very consistent in that approach. Our communications reflected that. In communications to not only families and kids, but also donors, we wanted everyone to know how Boys and Girls Clubs would be showing up for them and that gave people something they could rely on in a very unpredictable time."

The other element of success that Jeff reflected on was the importance of persistence. As any Executive Director can tell you, there are always going to be challenges and unforeseen problems to solve, but staying committed and focused on your core programs is a critical strategy to help deal with outside noise and distractions.

While Jeff underscored the importance of persistence, he also emphasized the value of flexibility. "You have to be open to iterating on a regular basis. Even if you have confidence in your basic programs, you must be open to evolving over time to stay relevant."

Jeff then went on to describe how The Boys and Girls Clubs introduced and evolved their new skiing program. Like many new programs, a funder came along and offered the necessary financial support to get this new program off the ground. "What we didn't anticipate was that it really wasn't the skiing that excited the kids at first. It was the bus ride." Fast forward a few years and the ski program became one of their most popular programs, with a waitlist of volunteers and board members who wanted to participate with the kids. They evolved the program to take advantage of those exciting and highly anticipated bus rides. Now The Boys and Girls Clubs utilizes important small group conversation breakouts during the bus rides, so that the most impactful work for the ski program happens before anyone even touches the snow.

Another aspect of program change and growth is whether to expand your programs geographically. Many national funders will encourage geographic expansion as a way to achieve scale and to align with their national footprint. However, not every program is designed to be scaled or duplicated.

The first thing to evaluate when looking to expand a program to a new region is whether or not there is an actual demonstrated need in the identified local communities. When looking at your mission and your programs, is there a need for your services and is that need being effectively met by other entities? Do you have the necessary infrastructure in place to achieve the same success in a new territory that you achieved initially elsewhere?

For Jeff Breslin, as new geographies were identified, a lot of pre-work was done to build new relationships to make sure that those programs would be welcomed and supported by the community. "The first actions really mattered. Doing what you say you're going to do goes a long way." That involved months and months of showing up and continuing to meet commitments so that by the time the program was ready for launch there was a familiarity and expectation that the program was coming and how it was going to positively impact the community.

The last element of program expansion for The Boys and Girls Club was almost an element of hope or faith. They had seed funding to get certain new programs off the ground, but there was also an inherent belief that, if they implemented their programs in the way they intended, people would show up, and the necessary resources to sustain the program would follow. "There isn't always a well laid out five-year plan for expansion. Sometimes you have to trust yourself and your approach and expand smartly based on that," says Breslin.

The Importance of Being Nimble

While many organizations use strategic planning or some other mechanism to serve as a catalyst to evaluate or reimagine their programs, for many other nonprofit organizations the COVID-19 pandemic forced them to make extremely time-sensitive decisions on programming in order to stay relevant and achieve their respective missions. Here are just some of the examples of how different types of programs adapted:

- Educational organizations: Many educational nonprofits transitioned to online learning platforms. For instance, Khan Academy expanded its online learning resources to accommodate the surge in demand from students learning from home. They also provided resources specifically designed to help teachers and parents navigate the new educational landscape.

- Healthcare nonprofits: As an example, Direct Relief increased their focus on providing personal protective equipment (PPE) and medical supplies to health workers. They also expanded support for vaccine distribution and information dissemination related to COVID-19 prevention and treatment.

- Food banks and hunger relief organizations: With the economic impact of the pandemic leading to increased food insecurity, organizations like Feeding America and local food banks adapted by setting up drive-through food pickup locations to maintain social distancing.

- Arts and culture organizations: As in-person events were canceled, arts organizations shifted to virtual platforms. Museums offered virtual tours, orchestras streamed performances online, and theater groups produced digital versions of plays and musicals to engage their audiences.

- Environmental and conservation groups: With limited ability to conduct fieldwork or host in-person events, environmental organizations increased their use of virtual platforms for advocacy, education, and fundraising. For example, the World Wildlife Fund (WWF) and other conservation nonprofits expanded their online educational content and virtual engagement events.

- Community support services: Organizations that provide services for the elderly, homeless, or those facing domestic violence had to adapt by modifying their service delivery models. For example, shelters for those experiencing homelessness or escaping domestic violence had to rearrange living spaces to comply with social distancing guidelines or find alternative accommodations for individuals to ensure safety.

- Religious organizations: Churches and synagogues that previously held religious services almost exclusively in-person had to develop streaming capabilities and build community through virtual content.

- Mental health organizations: Nonprofits focused on mental health and wellness, such as the National Alliance on Mental Illness (NAMI), increased their provision of online support groups, counseling services, and other resources to help people cope with the stress, isolation, and anxiety caused by the pandemic.

As the old saying goes, necessity is the mother of invention. What the pandemic showed is that the organizations that had the agility and willingness to pivot and adapt their services to a rapidly changing world were not only able to survive, but in some cases even thrive. While being nimble like this was not a high-priority skill for many nonprofits before the pandemic, this type of programmatic reimagining became essential during and post-pandemic.

Assessing Existing Programs

Many nonprofits offer an array of programs. They may find themselves asking if they are offering too many, too few, or just the right amount of programs to achieve their mission. This is a complicated challenge for many entities. As a new leader you may inherit a laundry list of legacy programs. How do you sort them out? What should stay? What should grow? What should go away?

Cynthia Figueroa is the CEO of JEVS, a human services organization in the Philadelphia region. She has been an extremely successful nonprofit leader in large, complex organizations, and has the unique perspective of having been both a funder and a nonprofit CEO. She encountered this very problem of needing to assess which programs were effective and which were not when she arrived at JEVS. She followed a legacy CEO who had been with the organization for 42 years, the last 25 of which had been in leadership. Many of the programs within the organization likewise had an extensive history.

"For me, I tried to help JEVS determine what was the thread that ties everything together. Once we were able to define the essence of our work creating sustainable paths to independence and economic security then we had the right lens to relook at our programs."

In the end, Cynthia and JEVS were able to use this refreshed understanding of the organization's mission and brand to assess its strengths and weaknesses. This informed critical decisions about which programs to expand, which programs to maintain, and, in some cases, which programs to disinvest entirely.

Understanding Program Costs

Cynthia learned early on the importance of developing a deep understanding of the true cost of the programs an entity puts forth. This is especially the case if you are involved with government grants, where operating margins are extremely thin and you are capped on how much operating support you can ask for. "It takes a lot of business acumen to understand the budget elements of a program. You have to know which programs are sustaining themselves and which are operating at a deficit and are being subsidized by the organization." In Cynthia's experience, "the healthiest organizations are the ones in which the most important relationship for the CEO is with the CFO."

When I consider programming costs, I am brought back to managerial accounting from my time at Wharton. In simple terms there are direct costs and indirect costs associated with every program:

Direct Program Costs

- Salaries and wages: Compensation for staff directly involved in program delivery, including benefits.

- Program materials and supplies: Specific items required for program execution, such as educational materials, tools, or equipment.

- Facilities and equipment: Costs related to the space (rent, utilities) and equipment (purchase, maintenance) used for the program.

- Technology: Software, hardware, and internet services needed for program operations or delivery.

- Travel and transportation: Expenses for staff or participants to travel as part of the program activities.

Indirect Costs (Overhead)

- Administrative salaries: Salaries for management, administrative staff, and support services that are not charged directly to the program.

- Office expenses: Rent, utilities, office supplies, and equipment not directly allocable to a single program.

- Insurance: General liability, professional liability, and other insurances.

- Professional services: Fees for legal, accounting, auditing, and other professional services.

- Technology support: Maintenance and support for organization-wide technology infrastructure.

Deciding what portion of your indirect costs to assign to a particular program is always a challenge. What is clear, however, is that not allocating some of these indirect costs to the financial analysis of an individual program will leave you with an incomplete picture.

Summary

Programs are where the rubber meets the road in the nonprofit sector. It's where we put our best foot forward in our attempt to have the desired impact on the population we are intending to serve. Nonprofits need to have a clear understanding of what is working and what is not in order to ensure that their programs are achieving their goals. Furthermore, they must study what it costs to execute each program, how to deliver their services in an ever-changing world, and how to evaluate current and future opportunities to ensure they are well positioned for future success.

Actionable Next Steps

1. Invite members of your board to attend your programs, with the goal of having each of them experience your work in person over the next six months.

2. Schedule a meeting with the heads of your agency's programs to ask them if they would like to be involved with the process of better understanding the costs of their respective programs.

3. Set a goal with your key financial staff members of completing a cost analysis of your largest program within the next month. Once you refine this approach, you can expand it systematically to other programs.

4. Schedule a brainstorming meeting with all your program staff over a casual group lunch to encourage them to share ideas about how your team can continue to adapt and grow your various programs. They may have more ideas than you think.

CHAPTER 7:
Building Your Evidence Base

Chapter Overview: This chapter dives into the various elements of program measurement and evaluation and why demonstrating your organization's impact is so important to its long term sustainability. It also articulates what is involved in creating a theory of change for your agency.

Evidence is power. Evidence is proof. For your organization to thrive, both in the short and long term, you need to be able to objectively demonstrate to others that your organization is making a meaningful difference in the population you serve, as described in your mission statement.

As previously stated in this book, there are over 1.8 million non-profit organizations in the United States alone. The amount of philanthropic giving is relatively constant over time. Competition for those dollars is real. "Winning" among institutional funders as well as other types of donors is a massive challenge.

One of the common threads among those who do excel in these arenas is that they can prove that their organizations are having the desired impact.

Measurement and Evaluation

Measurement and evaluation is the process your organization will undertake to try to quantify its impact. Measurement is the act of *collecting* data with the goal of demonstrating how much work is being done and what is being accomplished through your agency's efforts. It's about gathering concrete evidence of the organization's operations on its target population.

Evaluation is the systematic *analysis* of this collected data to assess the efficiency, effectiveness, and impact of an organization's programs. Evaluation interprets the data to determine how well the nonprofit is achieving its goals, what impact it has on the community or cause it serves, and how its programs can be improved.

There are ultimately two reasons why we undertake measurement and evaluation. First, it is important to know if our work is having the desired effect. Just because we have designed a program to help constituents doesn't mean it's actually working in the manner it is intended. Second, if it is having a positive effect, that data is the proof that can convince others to support our work so that we can expand our programs to help even more people who might be facing the same conditions.

There are a few important terms that are critical to the understanding and design of any measurement and evaluation program.

- **Output:** The immediate, measurable results of program activities, often quantified in terms of the volume of work accomplished. Examples could be the number of workshops held or children participating in a program.

- **Outcome**: The changes or benefits that result from the nonprofit's activities observed in the short to medium term. Outcomes are more specific than goals and are directly linked to the outputs. An example of an outcome could be that a child is now reading at a higher grade level.

- **Impact:** The broader, long-term effects of the nonprofit's programs on the community or issue area it serves. Impact reflects the ultimate difference made by the organization. An example of impact is that because of reading achievement, the target population is able to attend college at a higher rate than those children who didn't participate in the program.

- **Indicator**: Specific, observable, and measurable items that are used to demonstrate changes produced by a program or activity. They serve as markers for assessing progress towards outputs, outcomes, or impacts. An example could be a reading assessment done during the course of the program that tracks progress.

- **Baseline data**: Information collected before a program or project begins, which is used as a point of comparison to assess the effects of the activities and measure progress over time. In this reading example, this would be the child's reading proficiency before starting in the program.

- **Qualitative data**: Data that is descriptive in nature, often collected through methods like interviews, focus groups, and observations, which provide depth and context. In this example, qualitative data could be a child saying "I never used to enjoy reading, but now I do."

- **Quantitative data**: Data that can be quantified and typically expressed numerically. Quantitative data is usually collected through surveys. In this example, this would be a numerical assessment that could be used to collect the baseline data and post-program assessment data.

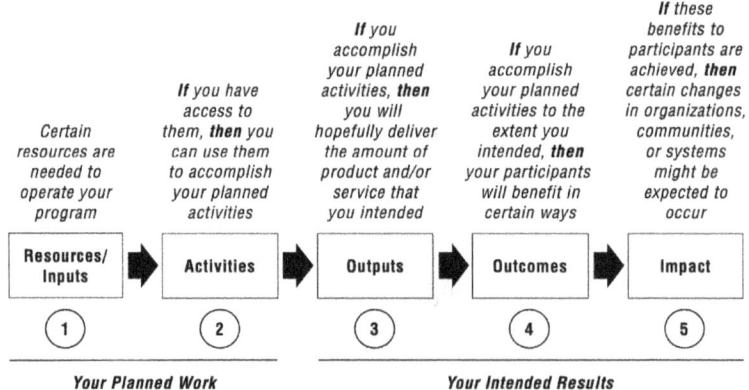

Figure 7.1. Breakdown of a typical Logic Model; *W.K. Kellogg Foundation Logic Model Development Guide;* January 2004

The Importance of Measurement and Evaluation

As stated above, measurement and evaluation (M&E) helps validate whether your agency is having the impact it intends on the people it is trying to serve. But the importance of M&E goes well beyond the efficacy of your work. In the conversations I have had over the years with institutional funders, they have described to me the processes they go through when considering who to fund and who not to fund. Many of them sort applications into piles: applications that are strong, those that are on the fence, and those that simply are weak. A common theme among those applications finding their way into the "strong" pile is the presence of logical and robust evidence demonstrating their impact.

The organizations that fall short in the grant review process may have a relevant mission and a good narrative. They may have strong, professionally managed programs. However, they simply fall short of being able to prove the effectiveness of their work. They may have a few key statistics, but those may be more along the lines of inputs (such as hours of programming provided or pounds of food donated to their facility) or outputs (like number of children served or number of attendees to their workshops). However, these numbers in and of themselves don't equate to evidence of impact. How did your meals served or workshops held alter the trajectory of the intended population you are serving?

If your organization's proof of that impact comes exclusively from qualitative data or anecdotes (stories and testimonials), then you may quickly find your organization coming up short in the trench warfare that is grant funding. These stories help humanize the impact of your work and therefore provide important context. But a major trend in the nonprofit sector is the importance of quantitative data to illustrate the difference nonprofits are making.

Doug Bauer, along with Greg Goldman, a fellow contributor to this book, was my introduction to the nonprofit world. Doug and Greg, arguably the greatest duo since Batman and

Robin, were teaching a philanthropy course at the University of Pennsylvania when I was looking to enter the nonprofit world in 2004.

Doug has been a mentor and a voice of reason for me over the last 20 years. As the Executive Director of the Clark Foundation, a grantmaker that is helping New Yorkers out of poverty and helping them lead productive and independent lives (they also have programming and a grantmaking focus in Cooperstown), Doug has a front row seat to the trend of measurement and evaluation growing in significance. In his view, the influx of a different breed of donors in the 1990s and 2000s brought in a desire for more quantitative metrics to help guide philanthropic decision making.

That being said, there must be an understanding that measurement and evaluation is idiosyncratic. How an arts organization vs a human services organization vs an environmental advocacy organization measure impact should be different. As Doug states, "You've got to learn and understand that results are adaptive and adaptable based on the organization and their circumstances as relates to their mission and the clients or communities they are serving."

In making funding decisions, Doug and his team take a holistic approach in assessing applicants. In no particular order, they consider the following aspects when evaluating potential grantees:

- The strength of their programs relative to their mission.
- The ability to communicate the effectiveness of their programs in a logical way.

- The experience and strength of their staff leadership team.

- The strength and involvement of their board. Not simply in terms of giving, but in terms of how engaged they are in the mission of the organization.

- The financial health of the organization. Especially during the pandemic, it was important to focus on organizations that were sustainable.

Collecting Data

Every measurement and evaluation program involves collecting data. Before you collect data, there are a number of decisions to make.

- **Who to measure**: The answer is not as simple as the people you serve. Your program might serve 2,500 people. Do you need to measure all of them? Is there a subsegment, or sample of this group, that adequately represents the larger group being served? If so, then measuring the smaller group will take less time and money than measuring everyone.

- **When to measure**: Most M&E programs utilize some type of pre and post measurement. A pre-study (before your participants experience your program) helps establish a baseline measurement. Baseline measurements are necessary to the ability to demonstrate future impact. A post-study (after your participants experience your program) typically involves assessing this same group of individuals against the identical measures used in the pre-study.

- **How to measure**: The design of research tools is its own field of study and we won't go into the weeds of the topic here. Surveys are the most commonly used for data measurement. Fortunately, there are a number of platforms available, like Google Forms, SurveyMonkey, and Typeform, which can enable your team to capture needed data.

- **What to measure**: In some cases, your organization may be able to use an accepted research tool that has been developed by others to help capture your data. For example, if your agency is involved with an aspect of social and emotional learning, there are already dozens of established measurement tools in existence that could be appropriate for your needs. Why reinvent the wheel? In other cases, your team will need to develop its own approach. The key is focusing your data measurement tool on the pieces of information that tie to your intended impact.

Deciding on a Level of Assessment

Rockefeller Philanthropy Advisors highlights a range of different levels of assessment your organization can choose when deciding how to properly determine its impact, each with their own unique nuances. They use an example of a nonprofit building a school in India to highlight the myriad of options an organization might have for its measurement program. They outline different types of measurement when considering the success of this type of project:

1. How many students are attending the school?
2. Are the students making academic progress?
3. Are these students going on to higher education?
4. Are these students getting better jobs than they would have otherwise?
5. How else are their lives better than they would have been otherwise?
6. Is the community better overall as a result of the new school?

What this example illustrates is that evidence and theories of change can have wildly different timelines and implications. Some of the answers to the above questions, like the academic progress of the students, would be characterized as outcomes from our definitions at the outset of this chapter. Meanwhile, a few of the latter alternatives, like whether or not students are obtaining better jobs than those individuals who didn't attend the school, would be classified as impact. Each of these options above would need different budgets and methodologies to obtain the required information.

Creating a Theory of Change

Every organization has a theory of change. Not every organization has it written down and articulated in a manner that others can see and understand.

So what is a theory of change? A theory of change, also sometimes called a logic model, explains the intended effect your organization is seeking to have on a target population. It is a macro if/then statement for your nonprofit…a hypothesis about how your organization is hoping to bring about change. There are essentially three main elements to any well-crafted theory of change:

- Before: The condition among the target constituents to be served as it existed before your organization came into contact with this population. From a research perspective, it will be important to document or quantify what the status was among this population without having the benefit of your agency's programs.

- During: A description of your "intervention" with this population. What programs, interactions, or other influence does your organization have on this intended community being served?

- After: The new state that the population now finds itself in as a result of having been exposed to your programs. Just as you will have measured this population in advance of experiencing your program, you will again be collecting data to see if your programs "moved the needle" in the way you had intended.

Rockefeller Philanthropy Advisors suggest that organizations ask and answer these basic questions when approaching what evidence they are seeking to collect[11]:

---

11 "Assessing Impact", Rockefeller Philanthropy Advisors, 2024, https://www.rockpa.org/guide/assessing-impact/

1. What problem is your organization trying to solve?
2. How do you think change will happen?
3. How long will it take for this change to occur?
4. How much money will it take to measure this change?
5. What will success look like for the population served?
6. What will be the signs of progress on the way?
7. Who else is working on this?
8. What assessment tools are being used to measure impact?
9. How much time and money is your organization willing to invest in assessment?

Thoughtful answers to these questions should create the necessary inputs and perspectives to inform your theory of change and help you make a persuasive case to funders about your impact.

While ideally you would have just one theory of change for your organization, you could conceivably have separate theories of change for each distinct program you run or population you are trying to serve. If you were a group seeking to improve healthcare outcomes for children in a certain geography you could have a theory of change directly tied to that aspect of your programmatic offerings. You would state what their significant health outcomes or metrics were currently, which of your programs were focused on improving those health outcomes, and then how that target population might be positively impacted by your work at some time in the future. Likewise, if the same organization also delivered programs related to nutrition and education, they could have a separate theory of change and measurement program which assessed knowledge and awareness of nutrition pre and post their program intervention.

There should be a direct link between your organization's theory of change and your organization's measurement and evaluation program. If you are seeking to make a difference with your organization's work, then you need to have a measurement and evaluation program in place that is attempting to measure elements related to the type of change you are intending. Measurement and evaluation is the "proof" that we are talking about as one of the 7Ps in your nonprofit branding arsenal described in Chapter 8 on branding.

Benefits of a Theory of Change

There are a range of benefits that can arise from your organization investing the time and effort to develop a theory of change. Some of those advantages include:

- **Collective thinking**: Experiencing a significant breakthrough in your collective thinking. The exercise of crafting the theory of change provides a space for you and your team to revisit and reimagine your programmatic approach to making an impact.

- **Gaining alignment**: Increasing alignment about how change will happen. Different voices in your community may have differing perspectives on how change will occur. The process of articulating your theory of change provides a space for your organization to obtain and synthesize these varying viewpoints.

- **Clarifying roles**: Better understanding the roles and expectations of different contributors. Change models can involve multiple stakeholders, and the theory of change can help to clarify those key relationships and roles.

- **Focusing resources**: Clarifying where to invest time and resources. The process of developing a theory of change may be instrumental for your organization to align your budgeting and resource allocation to meet the needs of your measurement and evaluation program.

Audiences for Your Measurement Program

Your measurement and evaluation program in concert with your theory of change are topics that can be used in different ways for different audiences.

- **Program staff**: The theory of change and monitoring of program impact can serve as a point of focus, like a North Star, for your program staff. The theory of change would highlight how their work is connected to the overall mission of your agency.

- **Measurement team**: Those in the trenches of your evaluation program can use the theory of change to refine how to go about this important work of capturing data.

- **Brand ambassadors**: For board members and volunteers, the data that comes from your measurement program will be the basis for the elevator pitch these brand ambassadors will repeat when introducing others to your organization.

- **Funders**: As discussed at the outset of this chapter, funders will examine the care taken in creating your M&E program and its resulting data to see how effective your organization is at generating impact among your target population. The most effective organizations are the ones who are most likely to receive additional funding.

- **Surrounding community**: In conversations with community members, your theory of change can serve as an educational tool to provide transparency about your entity's goals and how it intends to accomplish them.

Summary

To ensure sustainable success, nonprofit organizations must tangibly demonstrate their impact. Measurement and evaluation is growing in importance throughout the nonprofit sector. Your organization's theory of change should clearly articulate the intended effects of the organization's programs on its target population. Clearly demonstrating impact not only aids in internal clarity and alignment but also enhances the organization's ability to communicate its effectiveness to funders and stakeholders.

Actionable Next Steps

1. Contact funders that you know well and ask for feedback on your measurement and evaluation program.

2. Share your theory of change with your board members at their next meeting to give them a deeper understanding of the change your organization is seeking to create.

3. Contact organizations in other communities that are performing similar work to learn their approach to gathering evidence.

4. Review your portfolio of programs to see if any of them could be candidates to initiate a measurement and evaluation program.

CHAPTER 8:
Building Your Brand

Chapter Overview: This chapter illustrates various elements and strategies of building a nonprofit brand. It also provides insight on organizational rebranding.

For the last eight years, I've had the great fortune to teach Nonprofit Branding at the University of Pennsylvania in the School of Social Policy and Practice. I love everything about it. The energy. The back and forth. The pressure to perform and keep the students engaged. These are graduate students in an Ivy League school and they love the class. Student feedback is energizing. They find it practical and entertaining and many students stay in touch after graduation. What's not to love about that?

During the semester we cover a lot of the basics of nonprofit branding and I'll summarize some of the highlights in the coming pages. But more than covering course content, my ultimate goal is to get these future nonprofit leaders to begin to look at the nonprofit world through a branding lens. Hopefully you will begin to develop a similar branding lens as you progress through this chapter.

What is a Brand?

So what is branding? Well, part of the answer is in understanding what it's not. A brand does not equal an organizational logo. Visual identities or logos are a part of the branding equation, but when it comes to the nonprofit sector, they play a surprisingly small role. Most organizations don't advertise in the traditional sense so there is less logo visibility. Many organizations don't have a major physical presence. Typical marketing tools such as the logo are simply less important in the nonprofit sector.

Saying what branding isn't doesn't address the basic question. There are many definitions of branding, but the one that has resonated the most with me and the students is that branding is a collection of associations. That translates into the basic question "What do you think of when you think of _____ brand?" The brand is the summation of all of the emotions, experiences, and interactions that you may have with a product, service, or in this case a nonprofit organization.

- Are the people who answer the phone friendly and informed? That's part of the brand.

- Did the organization thank you in a timely fashion for a gift you made to them? That's part of the brand.

- Do you remember a story or fact that proves the organization is achieving its mission? That's part of the brand.

- Have you had a chance to attend a fundraising event or participate as a volunteer? Those interactions are part of the brand.

- Has the organization made the news for the right or possibly the wrong reasons? That's part of the brand too.

What this tells you is that brand management is multifaceted and interconnected. Success or failure in one functional area of your nonprofit can have serious consequences in a totally different area.

Think about a ubiquitous consumer brand like Starbucks. What do you think of? You might think about the green signs that you see in every community, or the music you hear when you are waiting in line, or the price of your daily caffeine fix, or maybe how long you have to wait for your beverage or food. You might also think about a story you've read in the news about how they treat their employees or the manner in which they acquire their coffee beans. The point is, you have to do a lot of things correctly to build a positive brand image. You only have to fail in one area to potentially destroy a brand image.

Farra Trompeter is the Co-Director, Worker-Owner at Big Duck, a full-service marketing and communications firm that has worked with organizations of all sizes from every aspect of the nonprofit sector over the last thirty years. Farra is also the host of The Smart Communications Podcast. Farra and the team at Big Duck help nonprofits use communications to advance their missions. She describes the brand as "your identity on the inside and how you're perceived on the outside." Unfortunately for many organizations, problems arise when there is misalignment between how the organization wants to be understood and the reality of how it is understood.

Many times the clients that Big Duck works with may be a "best-kept secret" who want to build awareness and be known by a broader audience or organizations that may be known for one thing but want to be known for something else. In some cases, there is a big gap between who the organization wants to be and the organization that people experience when they engage with it.

Branding vs Marketing

Many individuals conflate branding and marketing. While there is a relationship, they are very different.

Branding creates an image that represents, informs, and compels. Marketing is the strategy and tactics used to reach an intended target audience in an effort to drive some sort of response, emotion, or action.

Branding vs Marketing?

❑ Branding is why	❑ Marketing is how
❑ Branding is long term	❑ Marketing is short term
❑ Branding is macro	❑ Marketing is micro
❑ Branding builds loyalty	❑ Marketing generates response
❑ Branding creates value	❑ Marketing extracts value
❑ Branding is the being	❑ Marketing is the doing

Figure 8.1. Branding vs Marketing Comparison

The 4Ps vs the 7Ps

As an undergraduate marketing major, I was taught Kotler's 4Ps of marketing[12]. They are ingrained: Price, Product, Place, Promotion. These are the pillars or levers of marketing.

- How is the product priced relative to competition?
- What are the product's key features?
- Where can I acquire that product?
- What incentives do I have to buy the product now?

These marketing variables can all play a role in a decision to purchase an item or not. As marketers, we can manipulate or amplify one or more of these 4Ps to generate the desired response.

Those 4Ps apply to the nonprofit sector as well. We have a product. That is our mission and our related programs. We have a place (typically) where our services are delivered. We promote our organization through our website, social media, and other forms of communication. We have a "price" or a desired end result that people will donate to support our work. In many regards, all of our efforts will hopefully culminate in a purchase (donation) to our organization.

However, the nonprofit sector has an additional 3Ps that are different and potentially more powerful than what we might think of when we think of traditional marketing in the for-profit sector. Those additional elements are **people, proof, and process**.

---

12   Philip Kotler and Gary Armstrong, Principles of Marketing: 18th Edition (n.p.: Generic, 2021), n.p.

People

You don't market Coca-Cola through people. Coca-Cola doesn't communicate important messages to their consumers through its executive team or Board of Directors. We normally don't know who these individuals are unless some public relations disaster unfolds. Typical brands communicate key messages or events through carefully planned and executed mass media, social media, their product on the shelf, or consumer promotions.

However, people play a huge role in the marketing of a nonprofit organization. Think about it. Most smaller nonprofit organizations don't have a meaningful marketing budget or even have a marketing budget at all. Word-of-mouth advertising is critical. Staff, board members, and volunteers are many times an organization's voice to the outside world. They are the brand ambassadors. The challenge we ultimately face as nonprofit leaders is equipping these brand ambassadors properly to deliver the right messages. Are our staff, board, and volunteers armed with the right talking points, elevator pitches, or stories to bring our brand to life when they encounter someone unfamiliar with our organization?

Consumer marketing in the for-profit sector is very centralized. The marketing department or advertising agency sets the strategy and puts plans in place to tell the story. However, in the nonprofit sector, communications are decentralized and democratized. We rely on others to bring our message forward, and as a result, we must make a concerted and repeated effort to keep our brand ambassadors "on message."

Proof

Proof is another "P" that is critical to the success of building your nonprofit brand. Regardless of the rigor your organization places on measurement and evaluation, you must identify a few key objective metrics that enable you to demonstrate to others that your organization is having the intended impact.

The very first nonprofit Executive Director I met after I launched Pitch In For Baseball and Softball was Rich Berlin. Rich was (and is still) leading a phenomenal organization called DREAM, formerly Harlem RBI. It is a dynamic organization that provides youth the opportunities to play, learn, and grow.

Operating in East Harlem and the South Bronx in New York City, they had a clear sense of who they are as an organization and how they are helping the youth of the community. DREAM utilizes proof as effectively as anyone to demonstrate their impact and fuel their economic engine. While DREAM tracks a lot of data that demonstrates their impact, these two statistics crystalize their impact.

- 99% of the students who attend DREAM charter school graduate and 99% of those who apply to college are accepted.

Those numbers only tell a small fraction of the impact DREAM has had on the children who participate in their programs or attend their schools. This impact is even more impressive when taken in the context of the outcomes that other young people have in the community who don't attend their school. But sometimes it only takes one or two key pieces of data when you are in front of a potential partner or funder to tell your story.

Process

Process is the final "P" and one that also contributes to non-profit brand-building. Process might be your organization's secret sauce. How do you interact with your intended population? Does your program work better than others who are in your same sector, and if so, why?

One example of an organization where their process helps create a compelling case for the work they do is Shelterbox USA. Shelterbox provides essential aid, especially in communities impacted by a natural disaster. Their process of compiling essential items and their ability to get them where they are needed within hours of the disaster is an essential part of their brand story.

BloomAgainBklyn upcycles flowers to reduce social isolation in Brooklyn and throughout New York City. Given the perishable nature of the product they work with, Bloom Again's inventory management system and delivery operation is critical to their impact. Their process, once explained or witnessed, helps attract individual and corporate financial donors, strategic partners to make gifts-in-kind, and volunteers who carry out this well-orchestrated operation.

Incorporating people, proof, and process into your marketing mix creates an opportunity to leverage your stakeholders to amplify your brand. The immediate implication of having a range of people serving as your marketing arms and legs is the need for training of these various stakeholders so that they carry the right message forward.

- What are the key stories that embody your organization's work?

- What are the key impact data or statistics that you want to be retold?

- Do these brand ambassadors have the right tools to direct potential board members, donors, staff, or volunteers on how they can become involved in your work?

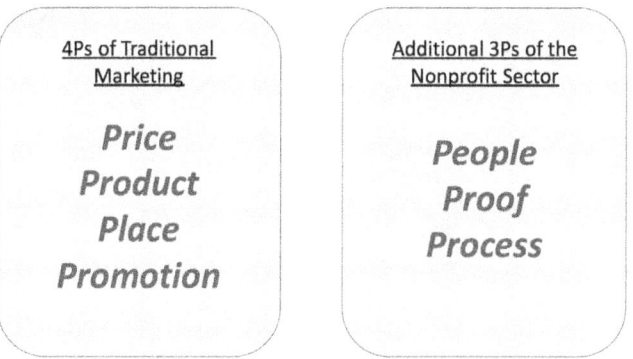

Figure 8.2. The 7Ps of Nonprofit branding, including both Kotler's 4Ps of traditional marketing and the additional 3Ps unique to nonprofit branding

Brand Building Takes Time

If you think that building your brand is a quick fix or a short-term plan to boost your organization, then think again. Brand building is a marathon, not a sprint. The way to win your branding marathon is through consistency.

The best analogy for brand building is outlined by Jim Collins in his book *Good to Great*[13]. He refers to it as "turning the flywheel." The thought is basically this: If you've ever attended a spin class and had the tension on your bike turned up, you realize how much effort you have to expend to turn the flywheel initially. This is what building your brand is like in the early stages. Lots of effort. Very little to show for it in terms of results.

The good news is that if you keep applying the same amount of effort that you applied initially, you will begin to notice how much more easily the flywheel begins to turn. You are now seeing the cumulative effect of the prior effort plus the current effort. If you keep applying this same effort you see how the wheel turns even faster. In fact, the wheel almost moves on its own with all of the momentum you've developed.

This phenomenon is something that I observed and experienced in my time as founder and leader of Pitch In for Baseball and Softball. The main message about our work from day one was simple: "We are the solution if you want to get baseball or softball equipment to kids in underserved communities. We can get them what they need and get them on the field, and we can do it quickly."

For the first several years of our work, this consistent messaging was heard and understood, but not much came from it. Over time, however, the clear association of our organization with providing equipment to kids and communities in need started to bear fruit. We heard from communities desiring equipment. We heard from grassroots equipment donors who wanted to

---

13   Jim Collins, Good to Great (New York: Harper Business, 2001)

make sure their gently used gear was put to good use. We developed partnerships with equipment manufacturers, corporate partners, and Major League Baseball teams passionate about this issue. We attracted board members who believed in our mission. We were building our brand.

Storytelling

Earlier in this chapter we highlighted the importance of proof to reinforce the value of your agency. But quantitative data are not the only way to demonstrate and communicate impact. One of the most effective tools to engage an audience in the work your organization is doing is through storytelling. Stories have a range of positive effects on those who hear them.

- **Connection**: Stories connect audiences to your mission. However unlike your mission statement which might be esoteric or academic in nature, stories are about real people and transforming lives. It is much easier for an audience (donors, potential board members, prospective partners, volunteers) to relate to a story.

- **Stickiness**: Things are described as sticky when they stay with us over time. They are memorable. You can easily forget a fact. You are much less likely to forget about a child or family whose lives were altered for the better.

- **Motivation**: The most common action nonprofits are trying to motivate is for people to support an organization financially. A powerful story is the surest way to create this desired action.

- **Content**: Stories make for great content. Whether it is word-of-mouth-advertising from brand ambassadors or your social media posts, stories often are the most effective way to engage an audience.

- **Authenticity**: Stories about real people build credibility and authenticity in support of your mission. When audiences hear compelling stories, they believe more deeply in your work and have increased trust for your organization.

As a four year old, Alex Scott began raising money at lemonade stand stands to help other kids like her who were afflicted with cancer. Her courage and her story captured the local and then the national media's attention. As an eight year old, her final lemonade stand before her death reached her goal of raising over a million dollars through her own efforts and from the hundreds of lemonade stands other kids held around the country to support her cause. Her inspiration led her parents, Jay and Liz Scott, to continue her work and form Alex's Lemonade Stand Foundation (ALSF). Since 2005, ALSF has raised and donated over $300 million dollars to support pediatric cancer research. It is one of the great success stories in the nonprofit sector.

A few years ago, Jay Scott came to my Nonprofit Branding class at the University of Pennsylvania as a guest speaker to share the origin story of the organization that bears his daughter's name. It would not be an exaggeration to say you could have heard a pin drop as Jay told Alex's courageous and inspiring story. Although Jay had likely told this story hundreds, if not thousands, of times before, the emotion in his voice was palpable. Needless to say, none of us present that day will ever forget about Alex Scott and her legacy of helping other children with cancer.

Rebranding

Rebranding or "refreshing" your brand has become commonplace. Many new nonprofit leaders seeking to make their mark will quickly choose this path as a way to show how they are making a difference. That being said, rebranding your agency is neither quick nor easy to do well. In many cases, a full rebrand will take 12-18 months before an organization's website and all of its collateral materials have been shifted to a new name or design.

With that in mind, I want to introduce you to Dr. Jocelyn Rainey. She is the CEO of Brooklyn Org, formerly known as the Brooklyn Community Foundation. Dr. Rainey is a force of nature and her energy and passion are something to behold. Shortly after she joined the organization, she felt strongly that a rebrand was needed because she believed that the Brooklyn Community Foundation wasn't serving all of Brooklyn the way she envisioned or reaching all its potential donors in the way that it should. It was still acting like a start-up, despite being in existence for over 14 years. She felt the organization needed to think bigger and be more of a reflection of the broader community.

I have had the pleasure of working with Brooklyn Org before, during, and after their rebrand, so I had a front-row seat to this change. Dr. Rainey's perspective on what made their rebrand successful boiled down to two important elements.

First, the rebrand wasn't about fixing something that was broken. It was about building on a strong foundation. She made sure that everyone who was connected to the organization—staff, nonprofits, funders, elected officials, and board members—knew that she respected and valued the work that the Brooklyn Community Foundation had done in the past. She wanted all of these stakeholders to know that the rebranding was focused on enabling the organization to do its work better in the future and to do more of it. The rebranding wasn't about change as much as it was about deepening their work and their commitment to the community.

Second, she brought everyone along on this journey from the beginning. While she knew she didn't know where the process would end up, she engaged staff, board, donors, and nonprofit grantees to let them know why the process was taking place so that they could embrace the new possibilities that the organization was about to undertake. Bringing everyone along sounds easy in theory, but not in practice. It takes time. Lots of meetings. And lots of listening.

As a result of its rebranding efforts, Brooklyn Org now views itself–and others are seeing it–as more of a thought leader and not simply a grantmaker within the community. Even for organizations that they are not (yet) funding, they are engaged in conversations and seeking other ways to build their capacity. Brooklyn Org overhauled its website and its messaging to reflect this bigger vision for the organization. It changed the scope and scale of conversations with individuals, corporations, and grantors who support the organization financially. It has changed the way it supports its community of grantees to reflect the broader community and not just certain pockets of Brooklyn.

In the end, rebranding wasn't about fixing a problem, it was about making the organization more relevant to the community it served. In doing so Brooklyn Org gives us some great lessons if you are thinking about a rebranding effort.

Farra Trompeter and Big Duck see a lot of clients who want to rebrand connected to a new leader or a new strategic plan, or both. "They want to grow. They want to expand. And they want us to make sure their communications reflect who they are. Before anything is assumed about how we are going to guide a client, we want to understand the big picture. This includes gaining familiarity with the overall organizational strategy and goals, reviewing the organization's current communications, confirming priority audiences and understanding their perceptions, and establishing the brand positioning and personality before trying to determine what the gap or rebranding need is. Sometimes the organization does need a new logo or name. But sometimes it's a more focused refinement, such as a new tagline and updating their messaging. We don't go in assuming every organization needs a complete rebrand."

Summary

For many nonprofits, their brand is their primary asset. Unless your organization has access to discretionary funds that enable you to have a robust marketing budget, you must rely on volunteers, staff, board members, donors, and other members of your community to carry your message forward. As nonprofit leaders, we need to arm them with the right facts and stories. Brand building efforts are like seeds that need time to take root and grow. While many organizations consider and potentially undergo rebranding efforts, they must understand that even successful rebranding efforts will take considerable time, money, and effort to bear fruit.

Brand building is a close relative of the phrase "stay in your lane." If you keep changing the messages you are communicating and you keep shifting the focus of your programs, your ability to build a clear brand in the mind of your target audience(s) is limited. Brand building is a function of message discipline and consistency. If you are trying to build your brand, then you are a believer in playing the long game. The benefits of establishing your brand in the minds of your potential donors, staff, board members, strategic partners, and other stakeholders can pay tremendous dividends if you have the patience and persistence to stay the course.

Actionable Next Steps

1. Survey each of your staff and board members and ask them what words or emotions come to mind when they think about your nonprofit. Patterns or common themes will give you a good sense for what your brand really means.

2. Ask the same question of donors, volunteers, and program participants. See if their answers line up with those of your staff and board.

3. Scan this QR code to listen to the inspirational story of Alex Scott to help demonstrate the power of storytelling.

4. Attempt to diagram or describe your program as a process. As you do, you may uncover important insights that enable you to tell stakeholders more about what sets your organization apart from others.

5. Create a formal elevator pitch for your organization. Boil down who you are and what you do into a maximum of three sentences. This can be more conversational than your mission statement even though it will say many of the same things. If you want to create brand ambassadors to help spread the word about your agency, tell them what to say.

CHAPTER 9:
Building Your Communications Strategy

Chapter Overview: *This chapter describes the importance of thinking of your community in terms of defined target audiences. It also talks about how to tailor your social media and communications to become more engaging and effective.*

Nonprofit organizations spend a lot of time and effort on communications. Communications are how we stay in touch with our community of supporters and partners. They are our voice. They are how people come into contact with us and how they learn about the work we do. Despite this, not all nonprofits have developed an approach to communications that is rooted in sound strategy.

Target Audience

Organizations utilize marketing because we are seeking to create a desired response from some person or group. We often hear the word stakeholders thrown around when speaking about nonprofit organizations. Those stakeholders might be our staff, the constituents we serve, our board, our donors, our corporate partners, etc. If we are going to put on our marketing hats for the next few minutes, it would be beneficial for us to stop thinking of them as stakeholders and to start thinking about them as a target audience.

A target audience is a group of people who may share certain characteristics, motivations, and experiences and therefore be predisposed to react in a similar manner towards certain messages. Traditional examples of target audiences might include men ages 40-59, families with children, pet owners, or college students. Without much effort we could list hundreds of examples of target audiences, but you get the point.

When we take this idea back to our nonprofit world, we can define these different audiences in ways that are very practical. Donors, volunteers, staff, and board are some of the most common ways that nonprofits think about their various audiences. However, if you think about these audiences more deeply, you will soon realize that not all the people within a given target audience are the same, let alone if we start to compare one target audience to the next. For example, existing donors, prospective donors, and lapsed donors could all be lumped together as "donors." Would that make sense? People who donated $5,000 or more for several years are likely different from someone who made a $50 donation this past Giving Tuesday. Would they be in the same place as relates to their level of connection to our organization? Of course not.

Beth Brodovsky is the President of Iris Creative, a branding agency focused solely on the nonprofit sector. She is bright, very high energy, and passionate about the role that marketing communications can have to help nonprofits achieve their goals.

When Beth engages her clients about their target audience, she asks them to do something uncomfortable and unconventional. She has them create an extensive list of all those potential actions that people in their community take that make their organization thrive. Examples of these actions could include liking a social media post to attending their annual gala to volunteering to making a financial donation. The list grows into dozens and dozens of potential actions. While our instincts might be to treat all of these actions as equally desirable, Beth asks organizations to try to think about the one desired action that could transform their organization. She wants them to ask and answer the question: "What is the one thing that if we could increase it by 10x or 100x we would be golden? Or conversely, if this one thing doesn't happen then we will struggle?"

Lovers, Likers, and Haters

With many of her clients, the most important desired action is to increase donations. Beth then asks her clients to identify those individuals who have taken this action six or more times. The individuals who have done so are labeled as the "Lovers" of the organization. She then draws a target with these individuals at the center of it.

It is critical then to study this group of individuals. Research focusing on the Lovers of the organization helps uncover what it is about the organization that resonates most deeply with them. When you discover the insights from your Lovers, you now have the cornerstones of your marketing messages. Beth calls this your "core message." What are the things that everyone needs to know about us? This core message should permeate all your communications.

So now we have the Lovers of our organization and we have placed them at the center of our target. Now we can begin to build out concentric circles from there. Who is the next group that, instead of taking a desired action six or more times, may have taken this action only a few times? We now have our "Likers" and we can research them. As you go further away from the center of your target, you may have people who stopped taking a certain desired action or who may have never taken this action at all. We can define this group as our "Haters."

A common misstep that many organizations take is to focus their efforts on converting "Haters" into Likers or Lovers and trying to convince them to take whatever desired action we are seeking. What history has shown us, however, is that this is likely the most inefficient thing our organization can do. While it is not impossible to persuade a previously unaffiliated or disinterested individual to support your organization, it is likely a long and inefficient use of scarce resources to try to bring them around. It is much more probable that we could get a Liker or a Lover of our organization to repeat that desired action than it is to convert or convince someone to do it for the first time.

Tailoring Your Message

Imagine trying to reach Gen Z community members and 60+ year old community members with the same message. Or using the same outreach to someone who knows a lot about your organization vs someone relatively new to your organization.

The inability or unwillingness to tailor our messages is another common misstep that organizations make. Given how under-staffed most nonprofits are, many organizations tend to send all of their audiences the same marketing messages. In fact, not only will they send the same messages to different audiences, but they will even send the same messages across different communications platforms even though the audiences on those platforms are vastly different.

It's not hard to understand how this situation comes about, but it is also very easy to see why it is ineffective. The flaw in sending the same message via Instagram or TikTok that you might send to your LinkedIn audience or in a traditional email seems obvious. While a message might have the right tone for one community, it could easily feel out of place in another setting. The ultimate test is to ask yourself the question: if a member of my target audience reads this particular message on this particular platform, will they know that this was meant for them?

The Customer Journey

A customer journey is a concept used to describe the complete experience that a customer goes through when interacting with a company or brand. This concept was introduced in Chapter

3 as relates to fundraising, but it bears repeating here in conjunction with communications strategy. This journey encompasses all the stages and touchpoints from initial awareness to post-purchase interactions. Here's a breakdown of what it typically involves:

- **Awareness**: The customer becomes aware of the brand, product, or agency, often through advertising, word-of-mouth, or discovery in internet searches.

- **Consideration**: The customer starts considering the product or service as a solution to their needs or needs of the community, comparing it with other options, and gathering more information.

- **Decision**: The customer makes a decision to buy the product or donate to the organization, influenced by various factors including product features, price, reviews, and overall brand perception.

- **Purchase**: The actual transaction occurs where the customer buys the product or service or makes a charitable donation.

- **Experience**: The customer uses the product or service and forms opinions based on their satisfaction, the level of customer support received, and more information about the impact of the product or the organization.

- **Loyalty and advocacy**: If the experience is positive, the customer may repeat purchases (donations), becoming a loyal customer and possibly an advocate who recommends the brand to others.

Chapter 9: Building Your Communications Strategy

Beth Brodovsky likes to talk about the journey in this way: "In the for-profit sector, you are trying to get people to buy something. In the nonprofit sector, you are trying to get people to *buy into* something." Beth tries to get her clients to think in simple terms. "What do we want people to know? What do we want people to feel? What do we want people to do? Once you can answer those questions, then you can build a marketing strategy to help people advance along the customer journey."

The concept of the customer journey is crucial for businesses as it helps in understanding the customer's needs and pain points at each stage. This approach allows companies to tailor their communications strategies to enhance the overall customer experience and increase satisfaction and loyalty.

When you apply the customer journey framework to the nonprofit sector (or any business for that matter), you can think about strategies to move someone from one stage in this journey to another. You have to know about something and care about something before you are going to do something. If the "something" you want someone to do is make a donation to your organization, then logically you wouldn't ask them to make a donation until they knew who you were and cared deeply about the work you were doing. While we all might want to skip ahead to the desired action, our marketing is needed to help move people from knowing, to caring, and ultimately to doing. Storytelling, which was highlighted in the prior chapter, is one of the most effective means of moving individuals along this journey. Stories bring our agency's impact to life and are often the most effective device for motivating members of our community to care and support our work.

Communications Vehicles

Website

For most nonprofit organizations, their website is their primary communications channel. In fact, most of our communications efforts are geared toward driving traffic to the website. I have been part of several website redesign projects and I've also consulted with numerous clients who have asked me to assess the state of their website.

While not an exhaustive list, here are the common challenges many nonprofits face related to their website:

- What vs. why: Too many organizational websites are focused on the "what" of the organization and not the "why." These websites are an exhaustive collection of every program, event, and moment the organization has experienced. While it is important for visitors to gain an understanding of what the organization does, it is much more important for them to understand why it does it. How are their programs impacting the constituents that they are serving?

- Too many words: Most websites are too heavily oriented towards words instead of pictures. Pictures convey emotion. There is a reason we have the cliche "a picture is worth a thousand words." Unfortunately, too many organizations choose the thousand words, and their audience either becomes intimidated by the wall of text or simply lacks the attention to read paragraph after paragraph. A better solution is large images with just enough words to capture the essence of the photo. It's ok to summarize key programs and initiatives. Your site visitors are really only seeking a basic understanding of who you are. When you have their limited attention, use it to inspire them. Don't focus so heavily on informing them.

- <u>Not enough focus on capturing email addresses</u>: Tom White, Executive Director, The Fund for Penn Medicine, at the University of Pennsylvania and a guest speaker at the Nonprofit Branding class I teach at Penn, preaches the importance of building your community through the capturing of names and email addresses. He professes the benefits of having a pop-up immediately upon visiting your site to incentivize individuals to share their contact information. Once someone provides you with their name and email address, you then have the ability to contact them with whatever messaging you want to deliver. The request for this information doesn't need to be invasive or complicated. "Sign up for our newsletter so you can be the first to know when new things are happening at our organization." It sounds simplistic, but Tom and many other digital marketing experts know the importance of continually growing your database. The larger your audience, the more likely you are to get more people to respond to opportunities in the future.

Too many websites don't place enough emphasis on trying to capture the names and email addresses of their website visitors. Yes, they may have a newsletter sign-up on some part of their website, but it isn't always prominent.

- <u>Designed for your computer and not your phone</u>: The final common flaw from a website perspective is not understanding how your website translates from a computer to a smartphone. Most design efforts are focused almost exclusively on how the content will be formatted on a computer. Images are big and content is easy to digest. Once that layout is approved by the client, the designer will take the necessary steps to make sure the site is translated to mobile and other devices. However, due to screen size and other technical constraints, websites don't always translate in the manner that we hope. The user experience can be very different. As content is increasingly consumed via our phones and not at our computers, overlooking this key design element can undermine the best website (re)design efforts.

Social Media

Social media is a common marketing tool for many nonprofit organizations. It is also an area poorly understood or utilized within many organizations. Board members will often inquire why the organization doesn't have a presence on every new platform because, as they point out, "social media doesn't cost us anything." From my perspective, the notion that social media is free is a fallacy.

Just because it may not cost anything to post on social media doesn't mean it is free. The time that staff dedicate to social media posts and videos is a real cost. There is also the opportunity cost of what they could be doing if they weren't spending time planning and executing social media.

Not all social media platforms are the same. We know this. LinkedIn is more professional. Instagram and TikTok skew younger. Pinterest skews more female. Facebook is an ever-changing demographic with younger people fleeing and older people becoming more of a dominant user group.

Because these platforms cater to widely differing audiences, we must understand that our messages, images, and other content on each of these channels must be tailored in order to stand a chance of being successful. Most nonprofits, however, don't tailor their social media messaging for the platform, and it's reflected in their results. Their Facebook and X (formerly known as Twitter) posts have meager if any engagement. Their social media fundraising campaigns fall well short of ambitious goals.

If we are to play in the world of social media, we first need to understand if our community of followers travels in the world of social media. Maybe our young volunteers are heavy social media consumers. If so, then wonderful. But if that is the case, then our content on TikTok and Instagram should be focused on elements of our organization that would resonate with those volunteers and celebrate their contributions. If our donors are older, as donors tend to be, then concentrating your fundraising efforts on social media might have very little impact if this demographic group doesn't rely on social media for charitable decision making.

There are many other important considerations for a nonprofit regarding social media. One of those considerations is how "conversational" we are as an organization and how responsive we are when people engage with us. Social media is not a one-way street. Think about Trip Advisor, the platform many people frequent when seeking recommendations and reviews for hotels and restaurants. Many restaurants respond to every compliment and every bit of negative feedback. They acknowledge when they fall short and promise to try harder in the future. They will also invite people to contact them directly if they are willing to give the restaurant a second try. In contrast, there are many restaurants who do not respond or maybe even monitor Trip Advisor. In those cases, negative reviews just sit out there unaddressed and for all to see.

Nonprofits who play in the world of social media must have a conversational mindset and allocate the resources to listen and respond when needed to positive and negative feedback. Social media is a dialogue. Sometimes it can be a pretty unhinged dialogue, but that is the nature of the beast.

Likewise, nonprofits have to look at what they are competing with on social media and ask themselves if their content can garner attention within that space. Of course, nonprofits put out posts that are meaningful to them, but if those same posts are objectively boring in comparison to what else is being trafficked on that same platform, then who is going to notice it?

Julia Campbell is a national podcast host and speaker who trains nonprofits on how to leverage storytelling, social media, and digital marketing to achieve their goals. Julia believes that most nonprofits fall into the misguided trap of thinking that they can reach their entire community when they engage in social media. According to Julia, "Many nonprofits view or expect social media to be their silver bullet that could solve their marketing and fundraising challenges when in fact social media requires great skill, effort, consistency, and creativity."

Julia sees two major trends as related to social media. Those trends are the use of short-form videos and the use of influencer marketing.

Short-form videos or reels are really the mainstay of how young people (Gen Z, and Millennials) consume a vast majority of their content. Teens learn about social or racial justice issues through TikTok. They see the impacts of climate change, gun violence, or the mental health crisis through Instagram. "Whether it's educational or entertaining, short-form video is the common language of those demographic groups. As a result, nonprofits are finding that it is much faster and more effective to attract an audience using content-rich videos on TikTok than to post traditional content on a static Facebook page."

The other significant trend Julia sees is influencer marketing. Influencer marketing is where brands or organizations try to communicate through individuals who already have large followings. Trust is at the heart of what nonprofits are trying to generate. The primary goal for most nonprofits is they want social media followers to trust them to solve certain problems. If they trust the agency enough, they will support them by telling their friends, volunteering their time, or donating their money. If your target audience is introduced to you through content creators they already trust, then they will be more likely to trust your agency in turn.

According to Julia, "What influencer marketing acknowledges is that young people don't trust institutions, they trust people.

If someone they know and like tells them something about a product or an organization then they will follow their advice."

When approaching social media, Julia teaches her clients about what she views as the four pillars of social media:

- Listening and research: When considering any new social media channel, nonprofits need to observe what people are posting and what kinds of posts are successful or not successful.

- Content creation: What content can you create that is going to work on this particular platform? Can you adapt your content to something that those consumers want to see?

- Community management: You need to be constantly interacting. Do you have someone ready to respond to comments, or to utilize hashtags, or to tag other people so that your messages will be amplified? One day you may be simply responding to questions about when your next event is, while on another you may need to navigate viral conversations about a particularly polarizing issue. Regardless of the type of interaction, you need to be ready and able to respond.

- Measurement and analysis: Organizations need to set goals based on whatever they are trying to achieve and then track whatever metrics are necessary to evaluate their progress and potentially iterate to improve their results.

Summary

Organizations use communications to encourage particular audiences to take certain desired actions. Understanding the various target audiences that make up their community enables nonprofits to tailor their message and deliver it through the most appropriate communications vehicle. Websites, social media, and other channels seek to create an emotional connection that hopefully will result in those consumers engaging with your organization. In the end, communications seek to motivate their followers to support their organization and tell their friends to do the same.

Actionable Next Steps

1. If the most important action you are seeking from your community of followers is a donation, then comb your database to see who has donated six or more times over a defined period of time.

2. Once you know who these individuals are, you can begin the process of understanding more deeply what it is about your organization that resonates the most with them.

3. Conduct a review of the responses to your social media posts over the last year. Seeing the results in black and white may identify some obvious areas that need attention.

4. If your organization hasn't experimented with short-form video in your social media content, set a goal of including video a few times in the next month to see how the response compares to posts that don't contain video.

5. Scan this QR code to schedule a complimentary session with me to discuss your communications strategy. I can do a preliminary audit of your website and give you some feedback.

CHAPTER 10:
Building Your AI Capabilities

Chapter Overview: This chapter explores the growing trend of AI in the nonprofit sector and some of the challenges and risks associated with utilizing AI.

People who have worked with me might find it a bit amusing that I am about to expound on technology. I am rarely an early adopter of new technology. However Artificial Intelligence, or AI, is so intuitive and so practical that I find myself embracing it more and more.

Advances in technology are part of life. Some of us may even remember life before smartphones. If we were to highlight some of the common benefits of new technology we might say that it helps us do things better or easier. While AI shares those characteristics, AI is more nuanced due to its far-ranging potential workplace applications on the one hand and the risks associated with AI on the other hand.

With that context in mind, how should nonprofit organizations think about Artificial Intelligence? Artificial Intelligence can be defined as a set of technologies that enable computers to perform a variety of advanced functions, including the ability to see, understand, and translate spoken and written language, analyze data, make recommendations, and more. It is meant to simulate human learning, problem solving, and/or creativity through an iterative feedback system.

While most major for-profit and larger nonprofit organizations have been using AI for years, my experience is that many of the smaller or grassroots nonprofits have yet to fully embrace AI. Maybe it is the fear of the unknown. Maybe it is the sense that they are too busy to try new things. Maybe there are some generational differences in terms of how older individuals adopt or adapt to new technologies. Whatever the reason, when I attend webinars or breakout sessions on the subject, there are more hands in the air for "I haven't tried AI" than there are for those who have.

Before we jump into a discussion about how you might be able to incorporate AI into your nonprofit organization, let's take a moment and clarify the different types of artificial intelligence that exist. For the purposes of this conversation, let's cover the two primary types of AI that a nonprofit organization could incorporate.

- Predictive: This type of AI is an outgrowth of predictive analytics or what might have previously been called business or data analytics. In predictive AI, data is used to forecast future outcomes. For nonprofit organizations, the most mission-critical use case for predictive AI is forecasting donor outcomes based on a donor's giving history.

Nonprofits can take advantage of predictive models to determine how likely specific donor segments are to respond to different fundraising campaigns. Predictive analytics can also identify the most effective channels, messaging, and timing for each donor segment to achieve the best results. Predictive AI tools can be costly and that remains one of the barriers to entry for some smaller-budget nonprofit organizations. To take it out of the nonprofit sector, one example in our daily lives is how streaming services use predictive AI to recommend content options based on prior viewing patterns.

- Generative: Generative AI refers to deep-learning models that can create high-quality text, images, and other content based on the data input.. Natural language processing, or NLP, combines computational linguistics—rule-based modeling of human language—with statistical and machine learning models to enable computers and digital devices to recognize, understand, and generate text and speech. ChatGPT is the most commonly discussed and used form of generative AI-a tool that lets users enter prompts to receive humanlike images, text, or videos that are created by AI. In contrast to Predictive AI, Generative AI can be accessed for free or for a fairly insignificant cost, making it more accessible to under-resourced organizations. For the remainder of this chapter, we will focus our attention on how Generative AI can be used within your organization.

Let me introduce you to Scott Rosenkrans. I "met" Scott listening to a podcast that he and his partner Nathan Chappell produce called FundraisingAI. Scott has spent the better part of his career counseling organizations on how to improve their fundraising outcomes through the use of AI. Scott's knowledge and passion about AI know no bounds.

Scott takes a practical view of why nonprofit organizations should use AI. He cited a 2024 study of social impact staff retention in which over 74% of respondents said they were seeking a new job or would be within the next year[14]. The main reason that they gave was that they had too much responsibility and not enough support.

Based on this alone, organizations should be using AI to lighten the burden placed on staff. The upgraded version of ChatGPT currently costs about $20/month. So for less than $250 per year, employees can be given the power to make their jobs easier, increase their productivity, and reduce their stress. We will discuss an array of examples of how generative AI can be used in nonprofit organizations in a moment.

However, despite this relatively low cost, Scott observes that there is still tremendous resistance for many organizations to dip their toes in the AI water. "Trying out new technologies follows a somewhat predictable pattern where there are early

---

14 "Social Impact Staff Retention Project", The Nonprofiteers, 2024, https://www.thenonprofiteers.com/sisr

adopters and there are laggards. It seems that many nonprofits, regardless of size, are in that second camp."

According to the Stanford University Institute for Human-Centered Artificial Intelligence research, nearly 80% of nonprofits still lack an organization-wide policy for AI usage, a foundational step for protecting data privacy, monitoring potential biases, and establishing norms around AI use in the workplace[15].

According to a March 2024 survey of 4,600 nonprofits around the globe, more than half of nonprofits say at least some of their employees use generative AI daily, mostly for proposal writing or content creation[16]. Yet, even as AI becomes more common in the workplace, many employees — and nonprofits — are just beginning to scratch the surface of what the technology is capable of.

How to Use AI in Your Organization

Nonprofit agencies tend to view generative AI as a productivity tool, helping with relatively straightforward routine tasks like completing grant applications and developing communications content. The agencies that make a commitment to utilize generative AI have explored various ways to integrate it into their day-to-day tasks. Some common applications include:

- Content generation: Nonprofits often use generative AI to create compelling content such as articles, blog

---

15 Sarah Di Troia et al., Inspiring Action: Identifying the Social Sector AI Opportunity Gap (Stanford University: Institute for Human-Centered Artificial Intelligence, 2024), n.p.

16 Nonprofits and Generative AI (Google.org, 2024), https://services.google.com/fh/files/blogs/nonprofits_and_generative_ai.pdf

posts, social media posts, donor thank-you letters, and newsletters. This content can help raise awareness about their cause, educate the public, and engage with their supporters.

- <u>Fundraising and donor engagement</u>: Generative AI can be used to personalize fundraising campaigns and donor communications. By analyzing donor data and preferences, nonprofits can generate targeted messages and appeals that resonate with individual donors, leading to increased donations and stronger donor relationships.

- <u>Program design</u>: Nonprofits can leverage generative AI to design and optimize programs, services, and interventions. By analyzing large datasets and simulating various scenarios, AI algorithms can help nonprofits identify the most effective strategies for advancing their missions.

- <u>Language translation</u>: Generative AI-powered translation tools can help nonprofits reach a broader audience by translating their content into multiple languages. Additionally, AI-based accessibility tools can convert text into different formats (e.g., braille, audio) to make information more accessible to people with disabilities and increase equity and inclusion in the process.

- <u>Data analysis</u>: Nonprofits collect vast amounts of data on their beneficiaries, operations, and outcomes. Generative AI algorithms can analyze this data to uncover insights, trends, and patterns that can inform decision-making, improve program effectiveness, and measure impact. With increases in impact measurement come greater opportunities in fundraising, especially from institutional funders.

- Chatbots and virtual assistants: Nonprofits can use generative AI to develop chatbots and virtual assistants that provide information, support, and assistance to their beneficiaries, volunteers, and stakeholders. These AI-powered tools can help streamline communication, provide timely responses, and enhance user experience all without increasing overhead.

- Art and creativity: Some nonprofits use generative AI to create art and multimedia content that raises awareness about their cause and sparks conversations. For example, AI-generated artwork or videos can attract attention, inspire action, and increase engagement, especially on social media.

- Training: Nonprofits can utilize generative AI-powered training tools to enhance the skills and capabilities of their staff, volunteers, and beneficiaries. Especially in leanly staffed organizations that may lack HR and/or training departments, AI-based simulations, tutorials, and interactive learning platforms can provide personalized learning experiences and empower individuals to contribute effectively to the organization's mission.

- Policy analysis: Generative AI can help nonprofits analyze complex policy issues, model the potential impact of proposed policies, and develop evidence-based advocacy strategies. By generating insights and recommendations, AI can support nonprofits in their efforts to influence decision-makers, shape public discourse, and drive social change.

Where to Start with AI

While some of the applications of AI listed above may seem too complex, there are numerous "smaller lifts" that can provide an entryway for organizations to experiment with and gain confidence in AI. Some of those simple tasks might include creating the following:

- Donor thank you letters

- Alternative subject lines for fundraising emails

- Refreshed narratives for grant applications

- Emails to frustrated members of your community

- Newsletter or blog stories

Scott Rosenkrans highlighted another relatively simple but valuable feature of ChatGPT. "The GPT Voice feature can be used to role-play how you might pitch to a major donor or handle the objections they may raise." Imagine the benefit of practicing what you will say before you have to say it in front of live donors!

The skill with Generative AI really comes down to learning how to craft the prompt that will shape the output. Small changes in the articulation of the prompt can yield very different outcomes with Generative AI. It is through the trial and error of prompt creation that you begin to uncover the magic of this tool.

Risks Associated with AI

While there are numerous meaningful benefits to utilizing AI, the integration of this technology is not without its risks. Forbes Magazine highlighted some of those risks and how they could be mitigated[17]:

- **Output quality issues:** Ensuring the quality of outputs generated by generative AI models is extremely challenging due to their unpredictable nature. One creative design from a ChatGPT model for marketing may align with your brand guidelines, but another may not. An advertisement developed by the model may be suitable in one cultural context but offensive in another. While a human might quickly discern such distinctions, the model lacks awareness of cultural nuance and may inadvertently produce inappropriate content. As a result, human review remains essential for assessing output quality.

- **Made-up "facts":** Generative AI models–while improving rapidly–still have noteworthy limitations, the foremost perhaps being the "hallucinations" when a model makes up "facts". The result can range from the harmless (misreporting who invented the cotton gin) to the possibly actionable (making up criminal accusations).

- **Legal risks:** Generative AI presents potentially significant legal and regulatory risks, as evidenced by cases

---

17   Bernard Marr, "The 15 Biggest Risks of Artificial Intelligence", Forbes, June 2, 2023, https://www.forbes.com/sites/bernardmarr/2023/06/02/the-15-biggest-risks-of-artificial-intelligence/

where generative AI tools have incorporated copyrighted material without the creators' permission. Moreover, the terms of use for generative AI applications often lack clarity on the usage of user interaction data for model improvement, which can raise privacy and security concerns. Additionally, the lack of transparency regarding training data in generative AI models may lead to regulatory implications, as demonstrated by Italy's temporary ban on ChatGPT over concerns about content, privacy, output accuracy, and age verification.

- **Biased outputs:** Generative AI models are vulnerable to the same risk of biased output as other models, based on biases baked into the data used to train the models. For instance, a prompt to "show images of corporate CEOs" might produce images solely of white males. Traditional machine learning models also entail these same risks of fairness and bias, but the generative nature of the new AI models heightens the risks when AI is interacting directly with customers.

Recognizing AI Content

As adept as AI is at creating content, there is a certain sound and feel to AI that can be identified. I came across a perfect example of this while teaching my Nonprofit Branding class at the University of Pennsylvania, when my students and I were practicing using AI to help craft donor thank you letters. With some minor adjustments to the prompts, we created three distinct letters, each more personalized and motivating than the one that preceded it. That said, they all started with the phrase, "I hope this finds you well and in good spirits."

Just prior to our next class session, one of my students (and a research assistant for this book) SJ Kounoupis told me how he had received a letter from his landlord this past week outlining a new policy in his apartment building. The letter started, "I hope this finds you well and in good spirits." The moral of this story is to treat the output of AI as a starting point for communication. Put it in your own voice and edit as you see fit.

Summary

At the end of the day, AI is a tool. Its output should not be accepted without common sense controls. From small tasks to more complex strategies, the thoughtful deployment of generative AI technologies enables nonprofit organizations to innovate, optimize their operations, and advance their mission in a rapidly evolving digital landscape. While still not universally adopted, AI can make the nonprofit workplace more effective and more efficient when used properly and with appropriate oversight.

Actionable Next Steps

1. Survey your own organization to see how readily AI is being used on a daily/weekly basis and if your staff is interested in learning more about how to use it as a productivity tool.

2. If you haven't already done so, check out ChatGPT. Copy and paste an email you are planning on sending into the ChatGPT prompt window and ask it to "proofread and enhance without changing the tone of this email" and see what happens.

3. Scan this QR code to subscribe to the Fundraising AI podcast hosted by Scott Rosenkrans and Nathan Chappell.

4. Scan this QR code to join Fundraising.AI on LinkedIn to stay on top of new AI tools and applications for nonprofits.

CHAPTER 11:
Building Your Team

Chapter Overview: This chapter underscores the importance of having a structured approach to hiring, onboarding, performance management, and retention to build an effective team.

Nonprofit organizations don't sell products. They normally provide a service in order to achieve their mission. In delivering this service, nonprofit organizations are very reliant on their staff to deliver their programs, manage volunteers, and communicate with donors and other constituents. People are what enable organizations to deliver on their mission and reach the members of the community that they are so committed to serving.

I was fortunate enough to start my career at Procter & Gamble (P&G) in brand management. This was a company that interviewed very thoroughly and, once they brought someone onboard, they invested significant resources in their development.

They were rare in this regard. Many employers view their employees as an asset that they are trying to extract the most out of before they move on. P&G believed that people were a source of competitive advantage and investing in them was a logical way to ensure the company's long term success.

My start at P&G helped shape many of my core business beliefs. But there were other influences as well, especially as relates to team building. In thinking about team building, it may be helpful to break it down into some of its component parts.

- Hiring
- Onboarding
- Performance management
- Retention

Hiring

There is an old axiom when it comes to personnel…hire slow, fire quickly. What this means in regards to recruiting is that we should be painstakingly patient in finding the right people.

A mistake that I and many others make when thinking about hiring someone is focusing on who we want. We may think about levels of education, experience, age, and even other characteristics. Over time I've learned that the more important questions to think about are not who, but what, why, and how.

- What are the traits or characteristics we are looking for related to the responsibilities and expectations for the position?

- Why is this individual interested in this job?
- How is this individual going to fit into our culture?

Some smaller nonprofit organizations won't have a dedicated HR team or even an office manager. So in these situations, most of the responsibility falls onto the Executive Director or CEO to lead the process.

There are many right ways to go about hiring and nothing I'm about to say is rocket science or cutting edge. As we all know there is nothing more damaging than hiring the wrong person. So no matter how much time and effort is involved in the process, the downside of getting it wrong is significant.

Every recruitment effort should start with a job description. Not one pulled off the internet, but one built from the ground up by you and other members of your team who know what the position will require to help the organization achieve its goals. Having a thorough, yet realistic job description helps set expectations and will ultimately be the basis for performance evaluation once someone has joined your team.

Interviewing is hard. Don't make it harder than it needs to be. Focus on those issues you think are critical to success.

- **Passion:** You are a nonprofit organization. Employees won't get rich working in this sector, so they better care deeply about the work you are doing. If you don't get a satisfactory answer as to what it is about your organization that inspires them, don't overthink it and move on to the next candidate.

- **Reliability:** There is an old expression in sports that someone's best ability is their availability. Meaning, they can't help the team if they aren't in the lineup. Is your candidate someone who takes a lot of time off, is sick frequently, or missed a lot of time at their previous job? For younger candidates, you may ask them how many days they missed when they were in high school. I want people who show up and value being accountable. If someone is late for their interview, do yourself a favor and send them home.

- **Problem solving ability:** I want to know examples (multiple examples) of how a candidate solved problems previously in their life. How do they overcome obstacles or unforeseen situations? If I know anything about working in the nonprofit sector it is that things rarely go as planned. I want people on my team who can roll up their sleeves and work through challenges. If they aren't comfortable with a little chaos, they probably won't be around for long.

- **References:** While it is hard to get anyone to speak on the record about candidates, do your best to find out more about them as a teammate. People rarely change. Find out what you can about how they performed previously.

In Chapter 8, you met Rich Berlin, the co-CEO of We Are Dream. Over the years, Rich has been generous with his time to me and I am unabashedly a fan of him and his work. Rich had grown and scaled his organization and the people on his team are highly talented. Rich's fundamental belief in people goes like this: "At the end of the day, it is your people who carry the whole thing. If you can't attract, grow, and retain your best talent, then you have no chance to be successful. Our organization is always trying something new. It's very entrepreneurial. So we don't always need people who have done the thing we are hiring them for. We are much better off when we can bring someone in where we can teach them our culture and let them grow into the job."

LaVonté Stewart is the Executive Director of Lost Boyz in Chicago. Lost Boyz helps Chicago's youth by trying to decrease violence, improve social and emotional conditions, and provide financial opportunities among the youth in Chicago's most needy communities. I'm not objective when I think about LaVonté and how he has grown his organization from a budget of a few hundred thousand dollars in their early years to over $2 million annually. He's someone I have immense respect and fondness for.

Like many of us, LaVonté has made good hires and bad hires over the years. In terms of the good decisions, he noticed a pattern. "It doesn't matter how good someone looks on paper. It's about how they connect with people...with other members of our team, with our youth, with the parents of our kids, with our coaches, with our other stakeholders. Sometimes you can observe someone, even as a volunteer, and you just know they are going to be a good fit. Getting people who connect with this environment have been my best hires."

Brooke Richie-Babbage, who you met in Chapter 1, advocates strongly for the use of a hiring rubric as a tool to reduce bias and increase consistency and effectiveness in your hiring process. In the actionable next steps at the end of this chapter, you will see how to find Brooke's podcast in which she goes into depth about how to build a hiring rubric that is appropriate for your situation.

Onboarding

Many times onboarding can be overlooked. Sometimes, whether it's hiring a new staff member or voting in a new Board member, we can be so relieved to have filled the seat that we don't put enough time and attention into helping this individual get off to a fast and productive start.

Rich Berlin believes that success for his team starts with a high quality onboarding process. For him the onboarding starts during the hiring process. "The hiring process will leave an imprint on the candidate. It's the first impression your organization makes. Then once you have someone in the organization, how can you make their start a positive one? It all starts with clarity around their role in the organization and goals. Those two things are paramount. Make sure they know what success looks like and what is expected of them."

To me, onboarding is really about putting yourself in the new hire's shoes and thinking about what they need to know and when they need to know it. By definition these things will be different within every organization, but the key is making sure you have frequent and open communication about how they are doing and where they need more support. Don't just pass by their desk and ask how things are going. That's not going to get it done. Have them debrief regularly on what's going well and what is still unclear. Make them feel comfortable asking questions. No one wants to look less than 100% buttoned up, but we all know that is not how things are in the early moments in a new job.

Performance Management

Procter and Gamble had a really structured approach to performance management and that is what shaped my thinking on this topic. P&G had certain elements of job performance that it characterized as "what counts factors" and your reviews every six months were tied to these criteria. It was a transparent process in that everyone knew what these factors were so there were few surprises in terms of how you might be judged. Training and development plans to address "areas of opportunity" were clear. These performance reviews also contained broad-based feedback from a cross section of teammates you had extensive involvement with. The overall process was an organizational priority. As I progressed in my career, I noticed that not every company shared P&G's commitment to performance management.

While there is no one way to establish the perfect performance review process, some of the common elements of a successful approach might include the following:

1. <u>Clear objectives and goals</u>: Align individual goals with the broader objectives of the organization. Ensure that everyone understands how their work contributes to the nonprofit's mission. Goals should be Specific, Measurable, Achievable, Relevant, and Time-bound (SMART).

2. Regular feedback and communication: Establish a culture of open and ongoing communication. Regular feedback sessions provide an opportunity to address issues promptly and reinforce positive behaviors. These can be formal (e.g., scheduled periodic reviews) or informal (e.g., after meetings or major events).

3. Performance evaluation tools: Utilize tools like structured performance reviews, self-assessments, and 360-degree feedback to gather comprehensive insights into employee performance. If one colleague says something positive or negative it could be an outlier. If multiple people are saying similar things it's a pattern.

4. Recognition and reward systems: Implement a system to recognize and reward employees for their contributions. This could include public acknowledgment, promotions, or other incentives that align with the nonprofit's values and budget.

5. Inclusivity and equity: Ensure that the performance management process is fair and equitable. Consider the diverse backgrounds of employees and how different factors might influence performance assessments and an individual's willingness to accept positive and negative feedback. (Chapter 12 is dedicated to the challenges and opportunities related to diversity in the workplace).

6. Documentation and analysis: Keep detailed records of performance reviews and feedback sessions. Analyze this data to identify training needs and opportunities for organizational improvement.

7. <u>Link to strategic planning</u>: Connect the performance management process with the organization's strategic planning. This ensures that employee performance supports the nonprofit's long-term goals and mission achievement.

8. <u>Transparency</u>: While there is no perfect system for performance measurement, whatever approach you establish for your organization should be clear and well understood so that everyone knows what to expect.

Retention

Nothing hurts more than when a cherished team member walks out the door. It's a gut punch. Replacing good team members takes a lot of time and energy. Hiring new people and investing the resources to bring them up to speed can be taxing and detracts senior staff members from focusing on achieving important goals. Smart organizations understand how vital it is to keep their best people. However, keeping good people is easier said than done.

In the nonprofit sector, some people will stay with the organization just because they relate so strongly with the mission and the population that the agency serves. In some ways, these are ideal staff members and the easiest to retain. As long as the organization continues to stay the course with its programs and primary focus and shares the impact of its work with its internal team, these employees will have all the fuel they need to want to remain on board.

Other employees may not be satisfied simply because of the mission-driven nature of the organization's work. For teammates that fall into this category, staff leadership may need to be more intentional and strategic about how to retain individuals such as these.

My conclusion from speaking with a range of leaders on this topic is that employees will stay if they feel like they are growing personally and professionally. They also want to be compensated fairly for their efforts. It may sound simplistic to put it in those terms but these are the themes that I've heard over and over.

The key to creating an environment where employees feel like they are growing is to involve them in their professional development plans. Embedding skills development and broader career goals into the performance measurement process can help hold both the organization and the team member accountable in this area. As leaders, our responsibility and challenge is to "walk the walk" and ensure that annual budgets contain sufficient resources for professional development. This will enable us to model and support these efforts by giving team members the time and freedom to develop their skills. It's not enough to say we want people to develop. We have to prioritize professional development in our culture so that staff understand that the organization is investing in them and their future and not just simply viewing them as an employee to perform a certain task for the here and now.

Summary

In most smaller organizations, the Executive Director is the de facto head of HR. Even if this is not an area where you may be most comfortable, the implications for not becoming proficient in all aspects of team building are profound. There's no secret sauce to building a great team. If there were a magic wand each of us would wave it. Your staff can and should be a resource that you invest in. Many agencies have very lean teams where individuals are relied upon to wear a number of hats. Building a structured approach to recruiting, onboarding, performance management, and retention will help establish a culture where team members feel they are valued and where their development will support the broader goals of the organization.

Actionable Next Steps

1. Scan this QR code to listen to Brooke Richie-Babbage's "The Nonprofit Mastermind" podcast episode published on May 21, 2024. She will help you develop your own hiring rubric.

2. Review your onboarding process to see where it can be strengthened.

3. Take a look at your performance review structure. Are there opportunities for other voices to be heard to give each team member a more thorough review?

4. Create (or expand) the line item in your next budget for professional development so that more members of your team have the ability to grow on the job.

CHAPTER 12:
Building Your Diverse Organization

Chapter Overview: This chapter spotlights the growing movement among nonprofit organizations to have staffs and boards that are more reflective of the diverse communities that they serve. It also touches on some of the terminology and other considerations related to diversity initiatives within the workplace.

There may not be a more "hot" topic in the workforce than diversity. DEI (Diversity, Equity, and Inclusion), DEIA (Diversity, Equity, Inclusion, and Accessibility) or DEIB (Diversity, Equity, Inclusion, and Belonging) initiatives are all prevalent in today's society.

Workforce diversity is the purposeful "recruiting, hiring, developing, and retaining" of employees who have divergent "backgrounds, educations, and experiences." This ensures that employees and leadership are reflective of the communities the nonprofits serve.

While diversity doesn't simply apply to the nonprofit sector, it is particularly relevant to it. Many nonprofit organizations serve constituencies where a majority of those populations are people of color and/or come from communities that are under-resourced.

Bringing a Diversity Lens to Your Organization

Many Executive Directors receive mandates from their board to "be more diverse." But what does this actually mean, and how can we achieve the organization's goals while better reflecting the communities we serve? In an article entitled "Why Diversity, Equity, and Inclusion Matters for Nonprofits," the National Council of Nonprofits also states the goal is to "start with honest internal dialogue that encourages your staff and board members to reflect, listen to each other and learn from one another's experiences."[18]

Greg Goldman is one of the first voices I heard from when I decided to enter the nonprofit sector more than 20 years ago. Greg has been a successful leader and C-suite executive in a range of high-profile nonprofits in the Philadelphia area. He now works with DiverseForce, a firm that specializes in diverse recruitment, development, and retention.

As you begin to consider the role diversity should play within your organization, Greg suggests that you start with your mission, and then you look at your community or your

---

18   "Why Diversity, Equity, and Inclusion Matter for Nonprofits," National Council of Nonprofits, 2024, https://www.councilofnonprofits.org/running-nonprofit/diversity-equity-and-inclusion/why-diversity-equity-and-inclusion-matter

constituency served. At that point, you might ask, "How does our organization and all of its elements...in its executive leadership, its community-facing staff, its board, and its volunteers actually reflect the community that we hope to serve?"

"We tend to think about diversity in terms of how it presents itself to us, primarily race," says Greg. "But there are multiple dimensions of diversity. Diversity obviously is not just race. It also encompasses gender and sexual orientation. A big issue that I think people are starting to think about more is age diversity at both the younger and the older ends of the spectrum. There's language diversity, there's intellectual diversity, people who approach issues from different perspectives in terms of their processing or problem-solving approaches. Thinking about diversity, not just in terms of how it might look in a picture of our staff or board or volunteer base on our website, but how it actually helps us in terms of functioning differently and better."

A common trap or mistake that organizations can make is to just bring in one individual who fulfills the desired diversity mandate or quota. At the board level especially, this type of tokenism can be seen as performative rather than genuine. It can also put tremendous pressure on that individual who has now been given the responsibility to solely represent an entire community or communities.

Greg Goldman suggests that a better approach, at least at the board level, is to bring in at least two individuals at the same time who help that leadership group better reflect the community or mission of the organization. "You can't hire one person or write a statement about inclusivity and feel like the job is done."

Some nonprofit boards may feel a tension between the traditional "give/get" financial responsibility of individual board members and the desire for the board to become more diverse. Young professionals or individuals who might closely reflect the constituents served by an organization that serves low-income communities, for example, may not have the same financial means or professional networks as their predecessors, making it more difficult for them to meet the historical give/get of that board.

Greg thinks that the traditional give/get model is a bit of a dated concept, and has seen a trend among organizations toward one of two different approaches. The first approach is to redefine their give/get expectations to mean each individual board member must make a gift that is "personally meaningful to them," rather than having a standard expectation that applies equally to all of them. While 100% of the board should make a financial gift as a vital demonstration of engagement and commitment to the organization, it seems out of step to hold everyone to the same demonstration of that commitment. It actually works against your diversity goals. The second approach is to create other governance structures, like advisory or community boards, where individuals who help the organization to become more reflective of the community are asked to focus on other aspects of the organization's strategic plans beyond fundraising. Regardless of which approach your organization settles on, it may be time to revisit the role that your board giving policy plays in your diversity objectives.

Diversity is not just an opportunity or challenge that starts and stops at the board level. Organizations are also under pressure and/or being more intentional about creating a diverse staff.

What does that even mean in practical terms? Organizations that have a wide expanse of ages represented understand that not every generation has the same approach to work or the same willingness to embrace technology. Staff from different backgrounds may have different and unique skill sets, and organizations need to figure out how to support the unique strengths and weaknesses of each of its individuals in order to build a team that can maximize effectiveness and impact. Another complicating factor to building cohesive, diverse teams is that employees now work a greater percentage of their time remotely. As a result, many team members simply don't know each other as well as when all employees came to the office every day and worked side by side.

Diversity Terminology

I want to offer a disclaimer. Language around diversity is changing by the day. By the time you read this book, the landscape and terminology will have evolved. Though the specific language you end up using may be different, the basic issues related to diversity and inclusion we cover in this chapter should remain relevant. An important and ever-evolving aspect of diversity is understanding what the various commonly used terms mean. Some of the most common terms that are used in conversations related to diversity are listed below:

- **Equality**: To treat everyone exactly the same. An equality emphasis often ignores historical and structural factors that benefit some social individuals or groups and harm others.

- **Equity**: To treat everyone fairly. An equity emphasis seeks to render justice by deeply considering structural factors that benefit some social groups or communities and harm others.

- **Inclusion**: An intentional effort to transform the status quo by creating opportunity for those who have been historically marginalized.

- **Bias**: An orientation toward something or someone, this orientation can be positive, negative or neutral; a bias can be informed by a previous experience.

- **Stereotype**: A trait and/or characteristic assumed to be true of all members of a particular social group.

- **Prejudice**: An assumption of knowledge about something or someone not rooted in personal experiences with the particular something or someone in question; prejudice is informed by stereotype rather than experience.

- **Ally**: One who is not (most) directly impacted by an issue but works in solidarity with those who are most directly impacted by the issue.

- **Marginalized**: A group or person treated as insignificant or peripheral.

- **BIPOC:** BIPOC is an acronym that stands for Black, Indigenous, and People of Color.

Another important term that is important to understand is "unconscious bias." The Oxford Learner's Dictionary defines unconscious bias as "an unfair belief about a group of people that you are not aware of and that affects your behavior and decisions."[19]

Unconscious bias, also known as implicit bias, is a learned assumption, belief, or attitude that exists in the subconscious. Everyone has these biases and uses them as mental shortcuts for faster information-processing. Implicit biases are developed over time as we accumulate life experiences and get exposed to different stereotypes.

As leaders, we may need to adjust our thinking as we become more familiar with these concepts and try to infuse them in our culture and our teams. While treating everyone equally may have felt like the right approach in the past, having a more equity-based lens might be the mindset you need to embrace moving forward. Likewise, we may need to look in the mirror and ask ourselves if we (or others) have unconscious biases that are impacting our views and decision-making.

Important Considerations Regarding Diversity

As a leader in your agency, there are many critical elements of diversity for you to navigate. When staff leadership and Board of Directors embark on a path to raise their commitment to DEI, what does that involve? The National Council of Nonprofits raises a number of important questions for agencies[20]. This partial list of strategic considerations highlights some of the decisions and challenges agencies face.

---

19 Online, s.v. "unconscious bias, n.", accessed August 14, 2024, https://www.oxfordlearnersdictionaries.com/us/definition/english/unconscious-bias

20 National Council of Nonprofits, 2024

- How transparent does your organization wish to be about the steps it is taking to become more diverse and encourage inclusive practices? How does your organization communicate its values to the public, to paid staff, and to volunteers?

- Are organizational values published on the nonprofit's website or otherwise shared publicly? Does it make sense for your DEI commitments to be inward-facing, outward-facing, or a combination of both?

- Do community, grassroots, or young leaders in low-income, under-served and/or marginalized populations within your nonprofit's community have a voice in your organization? Do they have authentic influence?

- How can your nonprofit open its board recruitment and staff hiring pipeline to talented candidates from among underrepresented groups?

- Is your organization's commitment to diversity, inclusion, and equity part of the orientation message for new board members and incorporated into onboarding new teammates and volunteers?

- Does your organization expect its collaborative and community partners to uphold its own values?

- How will your nonprofit assess the progress you are making towards your goals of diversity, inclusion, and equity? What will success look and feel like?

How Funders Enter the Diversity Landscape

Not only does diversity play a major role in the workplace of the nonprofit sector, but many funders, both individuals and foundations, are now taking diversity into consideration when they make decisions about who they will and won't provide financial support. Some of these implications include:

- **Donor expectations**: Donors increasingly expect nonprofits to demonstrate commitment to diversity, equity, and inclusion. Organizations that show progress in these areas may attract more support, particularly from younger donors and socially conscious groups.

- **Funding opportunities**: Foundations and grant-making institutions are more frequently requiring evidence of meaningful DEI practices as part of their funding criteria. Nonprofits that prioritize diversity in their staffing, programming, and governance are often more likely to secure such funding.

- **Corporate partnerships**: Corporations looking to enhance their own diversity profiles often seek out partnerships with nonprofits that demonstrate strong DEI practices. This can open new avenues for funding and collaboration.

- **Public perception and support**: Public scrutiny around social justice issues has heightened. Nonprofits that actively promote diversity and inclusion can enhance their public image, attract more support, and potentially avoid the backlash faced by those perceived to be lacking in this area.

A Work in Progress

While many organizations have outlined diversity goals in their strategic plans, and have dedicated resources to various diversity issues and training, the work of diversity is far from done. According to a 2019 Nonprofit Practices Survey, over half (57%) of nonprofits surveyed indicated that its employees are reflective of the community the organization serves[21]. However, fewer than half of nonprofits indicated having a "formal diversity statement, providing diversity training for staff, or having formal policies to promote diversity in their organizations." While the current workplace trends are likely different from this 2019 survey, these data points are a relevant benchmark on this issue.

Sample Diversity Statements

For organizations that are just beginning to focus their efforts on becoming more inclusive, one concrete step is the creation of a formal diversity statement. DEI statements can help signal the agency's commitment to this issue, help attract diverse talent to the organization, and help organizations build trust with the organizations they serve. Below are a few examples of formal diversity statements:

- National Geographic Society: We believe we can only achieve our mission when we actualize our commitment to diversity, equity, and inclusion in every aspect of our work. As an organization guided by science and innovation, we recognize that research shows the very

---

21 NonprofitHR, 2019 Nonprofit Diversity Practices Survey Results: 7-31

best ideas result from teams with a wide range of backgrounds and experiences working together effectively to harness the creative power and ingenuity of diversity. Championing all voices and ensuring members of the society community are empowered to bring their unique perspective and story to bear on our mission work is critical to pushing us to a brighter future.

- The United Way: At United Way Worldwide, diversity, equity, and inclusion (DEI) are core to who we are and what we do. United Way's mission is to improve lives by mobilizing the caring power of communities to advance the common good. In order to fulfill that mission, it is critical that our leadership and staff reflect the diversity of the many different communities we serve around the world, that we are intentional about including groups that have been historically excluded in co-creating solutions to community challenges, and that we apply an equity lens to everything we do, in order to ensure that every person in every community has access to the opportunities they need to reach their full potential.

- The American Red Cross: The American Red Cross fosters a diverse environment that is inclusive of everyone engaged in our humanitarian mission. Across the organization, the Red Cross aligns its mission delivery with a commitment to diversity, equity and inclusion (DEI). We embrace the differences and similarities of our workforce as well as our partners, suppliers and donors, to reflect the rich diversity of the communities we serve. At the Red Cross, DEI encompasses valuing the diversity of backgrounds, experiences, abilities, race, ethnicity, gender identities, ages, sexual orientations and cultures. We welcome all to engage with us–locally, nationally, and globally–to deliver help and hope to those in need.

Summary

Becoming a more diverse organization is a journey, not a destination. It is an ongoing process and not a box that can be checked. Creating a team—staff, board, volunteers—that provides different perspectives and has different lived experiences will inevitably lead to an organization being better positioned to achieve its mission and serve those individuals it is so passionate about helping. As our teams become more diverse, we increase the need for coaching and support that helps our teams address the unconscious biases and stereotypes that inhibit them from working together positively and productively.

Actionable Next Steps

1. Survey your staff to get their perspective on how the organization could improve as it relates to diversity.

2. Share some of the diversity statements listed in this chapter with staff and board to see if they would like to see your agency develop a statement that reflects your commitment to this issue.

3. Ask staff and board members if they would like to be part of a committee to draft an organizational diversity statement.

4. Create a line item in your next budget for a diversity workshop for your board and staff.

CHAPTER 13:
Building Your Volunteer Community

Chapter Overview: *This chapter analyzes the vital role that volunteers can play in a nonprofit organization and lays out considerations for the nonprofit to ensure that volunteer involvement is meaningful for both the agency and the individual.*

Some of my most vivid memories from Pitch In for Baseball and Softball stem from when volunteers engaged with our work. Some of those reflections include hosting families who collected gently used equipment in their community to support our mission or having our Board of Directors come to our equipment warehouse to help perform an annual physical inventory count of the baseball and softball items we had on hand. Another important volunteer engagement moment was working with the employees of our Major League Baseball team partners to prepare equipment for distribution within their communities. Each of these volunteer experiences was the definition of "win-win." The volunteers came away with a tremendous feeling of satisfaction and our team benefited greatly from their time and involvement.

Given the fact that so many nonprofit organizations are under-resourced, it is logical that many agencies rely heavily on volunteers to help them achieve their missions. Unlike the for-profit sector where members of the Board of Directors are (highly) compensated, nonprofit board members volunteer their time and talent with no compensation in return. (Chapter 2 explains the importance of boards to the sustainability and success of most nonprofits).

Nonprofits need to consider a range of issues before they should commit to incorporating volunteers as a meaningful part of their team.

- <u>Does it make sense for us?</u> The first consideration is really a reflection of the mission of the organization. Is there a logical role volunteers could play given the type of programming our organization provides to its constituents? For example, Cradles to Crayons is the nation's largest nonprofit dedicated to eliminating clothing insecurity for children. Donations of every kind imaginable come into the Cradles to Crayons warehouses in Boston, Chicago, and Philadelphia. Carefully trained volunteers check incoming donations for quality, sort them into a myriad of categories by age and size, and ultimately help pick out and pack donations for delivery to the children they intend to serve.

- <u>Do we have the capacity to properly engage volunteers?</u> Many nonprofits try to stretch their lean budgets by delegating work to volunteers. But does your organization have the staff, resources, and processes in place to ensure that volunteers are given the tools they need to be successful? Is the work they would be doing meaningful and will they have a good experience while doing it? If your organization does not have the infrastructure to deploy volunteers properly, what might have started as a good idea could have serious negative outcomes.

The Volunteer Value Equation

When engaging volunteers in the work of an organization, it is important to think about the motivations on both sides of this equation. What is the benefit to the organization to have volunteers? What are volunteers gaining from their experience?

For the organization, the most obvious benefit is getting work accomplished without having to spend its limited operating budget on additional staff. If that is the only way the organization is looking at volunteer involvement then it is being short-sighted. There are many other compelling reasons to incorporate volunteers into your organization.

- <u>Volunteers as brand ambassadors:</u> Having volunteers retell stories of how they've made a difference to friends, family, and co-workers helps build your community and potentially attract additional volunteers or other resources. The key for volunteers to become effective brand ambassadors is to equip them with the right talking points and other tools so that they can be comfortable in this role.

- <u>Volunteers as financial supporters:</u> While we must be appreciative of the time and effort given by volunteers, that should not stop us from asking them to engage financially. Volunteers have seen firsthand the impact of your organization. Why not ask them to help expand your capacity to do more? One of the keys to cultivating volunteers as donors is being intentional about how you stay in touch with them. For example, you always want to make sure to capture their names and email addresses so you can follow up with them again later. Don't just hand them a branded t-shirt and send them on their way until you have a way to contact them in the future.

- <u>Volunteers as future board members:</u> If someone has demonstrated a strong commitment to the organization as a volunteer and seems to have the personality or leadership characteristics to take on more responsibility, that could be an opportunity to discuss a pathway to a greater role within the organization.

- <u>Volunteers as connectors:</u> If the individual is a genuine champion of your organization, they can act as a bridge to connect you with key leadership at their respective companies. As we discuss in the chapter focused on partnership development (Chapter 4), a warm introduction can make all the difference when trying to secure a new corporate partnership.

Now that we have examined some of the ways volunteers benefit the nonprofit agency, it is also vital to understand what might be important to volunteers. By understanding the volunteer perspective, your team can make sure that it is providing these elements to your volunteer corps.

- <u>The desire to "give back"</u>: Many volunteers want to give back to the community in their spare time. Make sure you recognize their contributions and highlight how their volunteer service is impacting the constituents you serve. Talk to them about impact data. Volunteers may intuitively believe that your organization is making a difference but anecdotes and objective data can be highly motivating to volunteers. Share stories about how lives are being changed for the better. Facilitate their desire to feel good about giving back.

- <u>Meeting new people:</u> Volunteers are often seeking to meet new like-minded people. Be intentional about giving people the opportunity to get to know each other when they come together as volunteers.

- <u>Skill development:</u> Volunteers may be seeking access to new skills and experiences. Maybe your volunteer opportunity brings them closer to an issue they care deeply about. Maybe your volunteers will experience things they couldn't accomplish on their own like working with certain populations. Maybe your volunteer experience gives them access to a leadership opportunity or other skill that they couldn't gain access to in their day job.

- Recognition: Volunteers may not be seeking recognition, but that doesn't mean that they won't appreciate it. Many individuals don't get the appreciation they desire at work or at home. Thank people directly, or highlight their work on social media, in newsletters, or at your annual gala to send a clear message that their presence in the organization matters. Take the time to record short-form videos with your volunteers as they express what their volunteer service means to them and then play those messages back when you thank them for their time and support.

In the best-case scenario, leveraging volunteers to achieve the goals of the organization should benefit both parties. The organization gets important work done and expands its community through volunteer involvement. The individual volunteer gets recognition, a sense of giving back, and the chance to meet new people or develop new skills.

Involving volunteers is not always a simple process. As mentioned at the outset of this chapter, Pitch In for Baseball and Softball often utilized volunteers to help sort donated equipment or to pack equipment deliveries that were going to our recipients. On many days, the time we put into training the volunteers or double-checking their work far exceeded the benefit of the work they accomplished. What made the decision to use volunteers the right one for our organization, however, was understanding how important their engagement was to our overall success. These volunteer experiences helped grow our network of supporters and generate fresh social media content for our communications. In addition, our corporate partners wanted their employees to be involved in the community, and providing those companies with curated and meaningful volunteer experiences was a critical element to retaining them as a partner.

Leaning into Volunteer Engagement

Some organizations lean heavily into volunteer support to accomplish their goals. Two organizations that fall into this category are PennPAC and Compass Pro Bono. Both organizations provide pro bono consulting services to nonprofit organizations by addressing their strategic challenges. Their respective business models revolve around deploying volunteers which makes them particularly qualified to talk about volunteer engagement.

Jackie Einstein Astrof, who you met in Chapter 6, launched PennPAC in 2010. Jackie hoped to provide an opportunity for University of Pennsylvania alumni to give back to their communities through pro bono consulting in the nonprofit sector.

As the current Deputy Director of PennPAC, I have a front-row seat to see how volunteers can be infused at every level of an organization. PennPAC not only utilizes volunteers on the board, Advisory Board, and as consultants, but also in leadership roles in functions such as communications, volunteer assessment, and nonprofit selection. PennPAC is intentionally looking to see what "manageable chunks" of work can be entrusted to volunteers.

According to Jackie, "trusting volunteers is part of our culture. I think part of the reason we can trust them is that we know them so well. The other key to the success of placing volunteers in key leadership positions is making sure those roles are clearly defined and they get the oversight, mentorship, and appreciation that they need to be successful."

Similar to PennPAC, Compass Pro Bono delivers curated support to the nonprofit sector via professionals who donate their time as consultants. According to Deputy Chief of Staff Remy Reya, Compass Pro Bono utilizes a 5T framework to drive volunteer engagement and empower their volunteers to execute high-impact projects for local nonprofits.

- Training: Investing time and resources to make sure volunteers are equipped to be successful in whatever role they are asked to play. In addition, providing volunteers with easily accessible talking points so that they can be informed and helpful in their role as brand ambassadors.

- Toolkits: Organizing digital resources so that volunteers can efficiently gain access to information and training materials without time-consuming back and forth with staff members.

- Templates: Enabling volunteers to more efficiently perform their required tasks.

- Touchpoints: Creating a culture of communication through social media, email, and events to engage and celebrate a volunteer's support before, during, and after their service.

- Testimonials: Capturing quotes from existing volunteers to describe their experience to help bring volunteer service to life and to recruit future volunteers.

The 5 Ts of Volunteer Management

Make it easy for your volunteers to volunteer, from recruitment to retention.

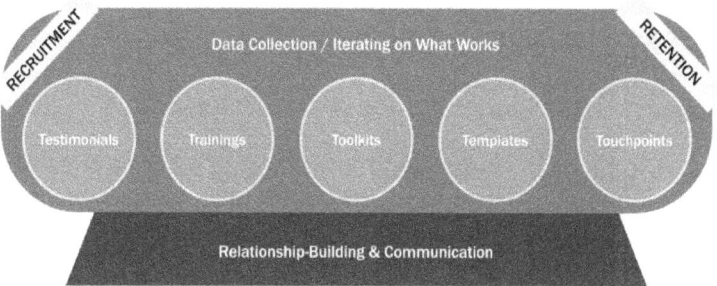

Figure 13.1. The 5 Ts of Volunteer Management;
Remy Reya; *Compass Pro Bono*

Firing Volunteers

Whether people are paid to do a job or not, sometimes individuals are not meeting expectations as relates to their performance in a volunteer role. Could you let it go? Maybe? But if the work is mission-critical, you shouldn't lower your standards when it comes to important work just because it is being done by a volunteer.

One area where this comes up frequently is with board members. Board members almost always join with great enthusiasm and high expectations. But as the months (and sometimes years) go by, their performance may drop off. They stop attending meetings. They stop introducing new people to the organization. Their interest and willingness to fundraise dwindles or vanishes altogether.

"You can't improve what you don't measure" is a quote often attributed to management guru Peter Drucker. In our desire to appreciate the willingness of our board members to be part of the organization, we often don't hold them to the same performance measurement standards that we would otherwise have for our staff or executives.

Creating clear expectations for board service, or any volunteer role for that matter, and then tracking how the individual is performing against those expectations is just smart business. In the case of Pitch In For Baseball and Softball, we created a simple progress report that tracked the following:

- How many board meetings did they attend that past year?

- Did they serve on an active board committee?

- How much do they donate personally in dollars or in-kind services?

- How much financial support did they attract through their contacts?

- Did they identify a new board prospect, major donor prospect, or potential corporate partner in the past 12 months?

- Did they attend the board retreat?

- Did they attend other organizational events?

Because of how fundamental all of these elements are to effective board service, we spelled them out in writing to prospective board members in advance of them joining the organization. Inevitably one board member fell well below expectations each year and this tracking mechanism provided a forum to discuss how they felt about their service. The most common reaction was feeling embarrassed and that they had let the organization down. I normally presented two options to board members in this conversation. First, they could commit to getting back on track, and then we could identify which aspects of their performance might need support for that to happen. Second, they could step back from board service.

Invariably, having them leave the board was the right thing to do, but I wanted them to have the option to turn things around. In this conversation, it is incredibly important to thank them for everything they have done for the organization in the past and to celebrate the lasting impact they had on the organization. I also pointed out that sometimes things change and people no longer have the bandwidth to perform in the way that they had hoped. Whether they decide to step away so that someone can step in and perform up to those standards, or they decide to stay and get back on track, either solution is a good outcome. What isn't a good outcome is having "dead weight" hang around and drag down the performance and morale of the board. Holding people accountable, even volunteers, is Management 101.

Organizations That Should Limit or Avoid Volunteer Engagement

We have just outlined a variety of ways to incorporate volunteers into your organization and the benefits of doing so. However, that doesn't mean that volunteers are the way to go for every type of organization. Here are some examples where the use of volunteers could present risks or challenges to the organization or the populations they serve:

- Healthcare and medical services: Nonprofits operating in medical fields, such as hospitals, clinics, and mental health services, need to ensure that volunteers are properly qualified and trained. The risks associated with unqualified volunteers providing medical care or advice can lead to misdiagnosis, improper treatment, and legal liabilities.

- Legal services: Organizations that provide legal advice or representation need to ensure that volunteers are appropriately licensed and experienced. The complexities and potential consequences of legal work require a high level of expertise and accountability.

- Animal care and wildlife conservation: While many animal shelters and wildlife conservation groups benefit greatly from volunteer help, these organizations must ensure that volunteers are trained to handle animals safely to prevent injury to the animals and themselves.

- Childcare and youth services: Nonprofits working with children and youth, such as schools, daycares, and youth camps, should be particularly cautious in selecting volunteers. Background checks and proper training are critical to safeguarding the welfare of children and ensuring compliance with relevant laws and regulations.

- Disaster response and emergency services: These organizations often operate in high-stress and high-risk environments that require specialized skills and training. Volunteers in these settings need to be properly trained and equipped to handle emergencies without jeopardizing their safety or the safety of others.

- <u>Services for vulnerable populations:</u> Organizations serving vulnerable groups, such as the elderly, homeless, or victims of abuse, must ensure that volunteers are sensitive, properly trained, and equipped to handle potentially challenging situations. Background checks and training in dealing with specific issues faced by these populations are crucial.

In all these cases, volunteers can be used in the right circumstances. Volunteers in specialized roles should not only meet legal and regulatory requirements but also uphold the highest standards of professionalism and care. Whether they are employees or unpaid volunteers, their work is a direct reflection on the agency and its reputation. Training, supervision, and clear roles and responsibilities are key factors in mitigating risks and ensuring the effective use of volunteers in these sensitive areas.

Summary

Volunteers can be an untapped and valuable resource for nonprofit organizations. To leverage them effectively, it is important to understand the commitment necessary to engage them properly, build a supportive infrastructure, and to celebrate their impact. Volunteers, especially those in leadership roles, should be held accountable for their performance and continually thanked for the impact they are making on the organization.

Actionable Next Steps

1. Attend your organization's next activity that utilizes volunteers to ask them why they attended and to thank them for coming.

2. Make sure your organization is capturing the names and email addresses of all your volunteers.

3. Highlight the work of a volunteer in your next agency newsletter.

4. Ask your board or legal representative to assess any exposure your organization may have as a result of your use of volunteers.

CHAPTER 14:
Building Your Crisis Response

Chapter Overview: This chapter covers how your organization can prepare to react thoughtfully in the case where it is facing a scandal or crisis of some kind.

There is an expression in business that there is no such thing as bad publicity. While that may apply in most cases, I'm here to tell you that in the nonprofit sector in particular, this is simply not true.

A scandal highlighting the mismanagement of charitable dollars or a personal indiscretion of an Executive Director, board member, or volunteer can destroy an organization if it isn't responded to with thoughtful and clear communication.

The poster child in this scenario is the Lance Armstrong Foundation. This foundation was a nonprofit rocket ship, which at its height in 2009 was raising north of $40 million a year to support those with cancer. At the time, it seemed that everyone wore one of their yellow bracelets in support of someone they knew who was battling cancer. Fast forward to 2012, Lance Armstrong admits to using performance enhancing drugs in his races, and overnight the face of the organization becomes a public disgrace as the bottom falls out of their fundraising engine.

There never really was a coherent response from the organization. Armstrong was so intertwined with the organization and the brand that there was little they could do or say to forestall the inevitable crisis of confidence. In the months that followed, it was not clear at all if the organization would survive. In the end, the organization rebranded to the Livestrong Foundation. It shifted the focus of its programming and is still around today, albeit with a much smaller budget, doing important work in the cancer community.

Maybe you read the Lance Armstrong scenario and think, that's really not a problem for us. We don't have a celebrity as the face of our nonprofit organization. We have a small budget. A potential public crisis like that is not something we need to gameplan for. You might be right. For your sake and the sake of the organization and people you serve, I hope you are correct that a public scandal doesn't visit your doorstep. While you can never predict if and when a crisis may occur, ignoring the possibility of a crisis won't help your organization respond if one does happen.

A crisis can take a variety of forms. It may involve someone being injured while in an organization's care. An organization can also be at risk for something they didn't do, like providing proper training to staff or volunteers, or conducting necessary background checks. Sometimes, the crisis can arise from something done to your organization. Maybe a high-profile funder misbehaves, bringing your agency's values into question. Maybe your database is hacked, compromising donor and client data. Your organization could be the victim of a ransomware attack. As former FBI Director James Comey said, "There are only two types of big companies out there. Those that have been hacked and those that don't know they've been hacked." Scandal can take many shapes and forms, which is why you must be vigilant and prepared to respond quickly if something does go wrong that can tarnish the image of your organization.

A Failure of Leadership

We don't have to look back very far in history to find a case where crisis communication (or lack thereof) has had a crippling effect on major institutions. Following the attack on Israel on October 7, 2023, we saw countless examples of leadership from leading U.S. educational institutions failing to respond effectively to accusations of antisemitism on their campuses, resulting in a myriad of negative consequences.

Despite virtually unlimited resources at their disposal, university presidents appeared before Congress and gave testimony and responses that had very negative consequences on the reputations of those institutions, their fundraising efforts, and ultimately led to several of these high profile leaders losing their jobs. So if large, well-funded organizations can fail to rise to the communications challenges they face, how can grassroots or less well-resourced agencies insulate themselves against the reputational and/or budgetary damage of a potential crisis?

Building Your Crisis Response Plan

Liz Wainger is a highly-sought communications consultant and strategist who has been on the inside of a wide range of unanticipated crises. Liz defines a crisis "as a threat to your reputation or operation." Throughout her career, Liz has seen the damage that happens to nonprofits–angry donors, loss of funding, disgruntled staff and board disengagement–who haven't been able to invest enough time in preparing for the unexpected.

It's difficult to predict the future, which makes it so challenging to prepare for any specific event. But lacking a resident staff fortune teller, there are still many things an organization can do in advance to better prepare them for unforeseen negative events.

According to Liz, there are critical decisions and conditions that should be part of a smart crisis response plan. She likens crisis communications planning to building muscle memory; the management of the process to plan for and deliver your key messages during high stakes and pressure filled moments takes time and practice. Here are some of the most important steps to consider and incorporate into your crisis response planning:

1. Identify who on your team (board, staff, or some combination) should be involved in managing, crafting and delivering the response, and who should not.

2. Build redundancy into your team, as the person you envision leading your response may end up actually

being the crisis. Or, that person could simply end up having some other conflict, such as having a health issue, being on vacation, or just being otherwise unreachable. Having a backup spokesperson ensures continuity and consistency and provides flexibility.

3. Create explicit and detailed communications protocols to avoid any confusion in a crisis.

   a. Who is going to speak?

   b. Who is not going to speak?

   c. What audiences need to hear from you, in what order and through which format? (Spoiler alert, you must talk to your staff first as they should not hear about a situation from news or social media.) They also need to understand how they should respond to questions they may receive from clients, donors, etc. Many times, incorrect information comes through the media not because board or staff members post on social media but because they talk to friends who in turn post or talk to the media and spread the story.

   d. What are the messages that must be communicated?

   e. What are they not going to say? Liz strongly cautions against the use of a flat "no comment," without an explanation. No comment can sound defensive and that you have something to hide or suggest that the problem might be even bigger than what it is. Instead, explain why you aren't able to comment at that moment or if you aren't sure how to respond, you can always lean into the proven PR approach of "I'm not sure, but let me find out and get back to you."

4. Workshop different scenarios. How are we going to react when each of them happens? Not every crisis is the same. Therefore you can't have a cookie cutter approach to responding to a negative situation.

5. Have key contact information and key documents easily accessible to your leadership team, especially whoever is designated to speak in a crisis situation. When a crisis occurs, there is a great deal of anxiety and stress. If your team has to thumb through a thick binder to figure out what to do, it is likely not to be effective and may only create more confusion. Create a condensed and clear executive summary that will point key team members in the right direction if a negative event occurs. Use bullet points and charts to make information easy to read.

6. Be sensitive to the fact that not everyone in your community may speak English. Make sure you have access to translators so that key pieces of information are disseminated in the languages that your stakeholders understand.

7. Have a plan for how to use or limit social media during the crisis. The best laid response plans could easily be undone by an unanticipated tweet or Instagram post. Sometimes a response on social media can simply inflame a situation. It is important to have someone monitoring the conversation on social media and to

make decisions about when, how and if you should respond. You don't want to have damaging misinformation out there unchallenged.

8. Create sample statements for each scenario that you workshop. While these statements will likely need to be edited on the fly, they provide a place to start. For example:

    a. "It would be inappropriate for me to comment at this time as we are still gathering more information."

    b. "I'm not the right person to talk to you about that, but here is who I can direct you to."

    c. "I really can't discuss _____, but here is what I can tell you…"

9. Be human. Express pain and empathy without taking the blame for the event. People need to hear that you understand they may be hurting or angry.

10. Identify additional perspectives (i.e. tech or legal) that might need to be consulted before any statements are disseminated.

11. Have regular meetings with your executive team–at least twice a year--to review your crisis communications plans and protocols. These reviews are where you can build the communications muscle memory that is so important.

12. If a crisis does occur, do an after event review to see what you did well and what you could have done better. This

isn't to assign blame. This is to improve your protocols and your process in the event something happens again in the future.

Striking the Right Tone in Your Communications

Let's assume you have protocols in place and a plan for how to roll out your crisis communications. What do you actually say and how do you say it? To expand on this, let's look back to our university presidents and examine where they may have come up short, and why.

As many pundits have speculated, it appears that these leaders were prepped for their appearance before Congress by lawyers rather than communications experts. Members of Congress wanted to probe how universities were responding to antisemitic rhetoric and actions on their campuses. The university presidents were prepared to address the letter of the law as relates to free speech, the right to assemble, and the limits of where their various codes of conduct started and stopped. What they failed to do was to understand that this was not a court of law. It was as Liz Wainger rightly describes "the court of public opinion." They failed to express empathy or a basic understanding of how their words would be played and replayed for the hours and days to come. They tried to apply a rational model to an emotional situation. As a result, in the very high stakes court of public opinion, they failed the leadership test.

Granted, most of us won't be appearing before Congress or be subjected to the kind of scrutiny that these leaders faced. That does not mean we can't learn from their mistakes and prepare ourselves and our organizations to better address the audiences who are critical to our success and impact.

Given multiple opportunities, they didn't say any number of things that could have been considered clear, strong, and compassionate. For example, they could have said, "Calling for genocide is threatening and we will deal with it swiftly if it occurs on our campus." Alternatively, they could have said, "Racism in any form is bullying and unacceptable and in clear violation of our code of conduct." To make it more personal and less unfeeling, they could have said, "This is offensive to me and I understand people are hurting and I am going to do everything in my power to make sure that all students and faculty feel safe on campus." Instead they equivocated and pontificated. They failed to understand the pain or embarrassment that students, alumni, and donors were feeling. They missed the opportunity to speak from the heart to the array of stakeholders who wanted clarity, reassurance, and empathy.

Summary

Your staff and board leaders should consider risk management a crucial part of their jobs, and crisis management falls firmly under that umbrella. While your organization may not possess a fully functioning crystal ball, it can certainly identify a few likely scenarios that could occur given the nature of its work. Identifying who will and won't be representing your organization in these situations, what audiences they will address and when, and what staff can and cannot say when confronted is the type of crucial preparation that will pay dividends in the event of a crisis.

Actionable Next Steps

1. Encourage the board to form a crisis response committee that would be supported by staff leadership.

2. Even without a formal response plan, outline the basics of who will speak and who will not speak on behalf of the organization in the event of a crisis.

3. Ask the board if they have contacts within their network who could help the organization with its communications during a crisis.

4. Make sure you communicate with your staff. They need to understand the protocols and the importance of receiving information directly from the organization, not from outside sources.

5. Follow Liz Wainger or other communications specialists on LinkedIn.

CHAPTER 15:
Building Your Exit Strategy

Chapter Overview: *This chapter examines how a nonprofit might prepare for and manage through a change in its staff leadership.*

There is an expression that says "all good things must come to an end" and so is the case with any role as the Executive Director or CEO of a nonprofit organization. Assuming your leaving of the organization is voluntary and intentional, rather than the result of some event or crisis that forces you out the door, your final chapter can be to ensure that the organization has a well thought out approach to bringing in its next leader.

As you may recall from Chapter 2 highlighting the board's responsibilities, hiring the staff leader of the organization is a key responsibility of the board. As a result, succession planning also falls under the auspices of the board. The board's decision on who will carry out the day-to-day leadership of the agency will have drastic and long-term implications on the sustainability of the organization.

While there may be nuanced differences between identifying a successor to a founding CEO vs some other executive leader, as well as differences between addressing a scheduled vs sudden leadership exit, this chapter will identify key elements of the process which can apply universally to any such transitions.

Creating a Hiring Committee

After the CEO has expressed their intention to leave the organization at some point in the future, the most likely response (in addition to potentially some panic) is for the board to create a hiring committee. This committee will both outline a hiring process and then subsequently play a leading role in the final decision of choosing the new chief executive. While every member of the board may want to have a voice in this work, it is unlikely that the full board will have the capacity to dedicate the full amount of time necessary to do it well. Beyond that, trying to engage the full board at every critical step in this process seems unwieldy, assuming the board has more than five members.

Key Decisions in a Hiring Process

Regardless of the formality or length of the hiring process, there are a number of important decisions a board and its hiring committee will likely consider:

- **Evaluating internal candidates:** A likely question that the board will entertain is "do we already have someone on staff who could take over?" In many small to mid-sized organizations, there simply aren't a large pool of seasoned staff members who might have the requisite skills and experience to make the leap into the chief executive role. While the board may want to invite current staff to "throw their hat in the ring" to be the new leader, the board should also consider the implications of an internal candidate being rejected in favor of an outside choice. Will the existing staff member be resentful and consider moving on to a new opportunity?

- **Compensation level:** Just because the current Executive Director is being compensated at a certain level of pay and benefits does not mean that it is in step with what prospective candidates would see as suitable given the demands of the job. Conducting a compensation audit for similarly sized organizations in your geographic region can help inform the board's expectations about what level of experience they might expect based on the compensation they are offering the new leader. While it is not as simple as "you get what you pay for," determining the compensation level can be a huge variable in any hiring process.

- **The role of diversity in a hiring decision:** Many boards utilize a leadership change as an opportunity to redefine their organization in terms of how its face reflects the community it serves. This can be particularly relevant for nonprofits who provide services or advocacy primarily to communities of color. The pressure or desire to "be a more diverse organization" can often be a huge determinant of which candidates a hiring committee prioritizes during the vetting process. This is a complex issue for many organizations, but recent trends would suggest that it is playing an increasingly important role in new leadership hiring decisions.

- **Retaining a search firm:** One of the most fundamental decisions a board will wrestle with is whether to manage the hiring process internally or to retain the services of an executive search firm. Some of the key considerations might include:

    Time to manage the process: Creating the job description, screening candidate resumes and cover letters, and conducting preliminary interviews all take time. Do you feel confident that the members of your internal hiring team have the time and expertise to manage these workstreams?

    Lack of hiring experience: Interviewing and making the right final decision on a candidate are skills that should not be left in the hands of individuals who don't have this background. If this lack of hiring experience is a factor within your organization, leaning into the experience of a search firm is one strategy to overcome this concern.

    Cost of bringing in outside consultants: Fee structures for executive search firms can differ greatly, but regardless of how it is structured, your organization may not have the resources needed to bring in outside support. It may be necessary for your board/finance committee to look at the extraordinary nature of this expense to see whether reworking the budget is the right thing for your agency to do.

Identifying the best talent: Many search firms have access to deep pools of experienced candidates. Moreover, they may have access to talent that is outside of your geographic reach. If your board is not confident that it can draw from and identify the best talent, then a search firm could be a viable solution to overcome this situation.

Creating a diverse candidate pool: If your organization is seeking a diverse candidate to fill this role, search firms can sometimes be a more effective mechanism to identify qualified candidates than if the organization oversees the process themselves. Given that many CEO roles are filled through word-of-mouth and networking, if your current board leadership lacks diversity then their networks may lack diversity as well. Outside agencies may have reach to other candidates and networks that current members of your board do not.

Legal considerations: If your board is concerned about avoiding any legal aspects of the hiring process, bringing in an agency that has a structured process and employment practice liability insurance is one way to mitigate this risk.

Considering Interim Leadership

Interim leadership is a strategy whereby a firm hires someone, knowing that they are not going to be the permanent solution to fill a specific role, to address issues that will better prepare the organization for a permanent hire. This approach is an alternative that is gaining increasing popularity in the executive hiring process. One firm that helps place and support interim leaders in the nonprofit sector is Interim Executive Solutions (IES). David Harris, the Managing Director of IES, believes that one of the reasons that interim leadership is gaining traction is that "in many organizations the board is too in the weeds to objectively know what the organization really needs long term to be successful in terms of leadership skills. In other situations, the board is too disconnected from the actual work of the organization to know how to proceed in terms of a new leader's style."

Harris says that what an interim leader does is to "hold up a mirror to the organization" and help assess what's really going on: what is working well and what is not, what resources the staff needs that they are not receiving, and what the board can do to facilitate their work and help provide those resources.

Unlike a permanent leadership hire, a good interim leader can focus on listening and collaborating to help the permanent staff get their work done more effectively and sustainably, ultimately helping create a more stable environment for a new permanent chief executive whenever they do arrive.

Interim leadership can be a particularly smart strategy when an Executive Director leaves an agency suddenly for whatever reason, but it can also be very valuable following a long-time leader who might not have focused on the organization's infrastructure. While hiring an interim leader ultimately delays finding the new long-term leader of the organization, interim leadership can provide stability in the near term and can give the board time and insight as it develops its long-term hiring process.

Creating a New Leadership Model

The prospect of hiring a new leader has led some organizations and their boards to look at some alternatives to the traditional CEO model. One model that is gaining popularity in the nonprofit sector is the co-CEO model. While the prospect of hiring two new leaders may be daunting, the co-CEO model may be the one that best fits the diverse skills and experience that the leadership role demands. This approach could reduce the pressure to find the "perfect candidate" and could also be a potential pathway to elevate an existing staff member to take on greater responsibility.

Preparing for a New Leader

As Tim Wolfred states so clearly in his book *Managing Executive Transitions*, the board should ask itself, "Where are we going and who is the best leader to get us there?"[22] These questions could prompt the organization to review or refresh its strategic plan to make sure it has a clear and well-articulated vision for the future. In doing so, the board will be able to create an efficient process that clarifies the strategic priorities of the agency,

---

22 Tim Wolfred, Managing Executive Transitions: A Guide for Nonprofits (Minnesota: Fieldstone Alliance, 2009), n.p.

including what skills and leadership style will be required to help it thrive and achieve its outlined goals.

Colin Weil is the former Executive Director of B'Nai Jeshurun in New York City. It happens to be the synagogue where my family and I are members, and I can personally attest to the fact that Colin led this vibrant and diverse organization with tremendous grace and empathy during his eight-year tenure there. As someone who just left a leadership role, Colin feels that one of the most important elements of a leadership transition is for the organization to be "reflective and introspective" before launching into the hiring process. In doing so, the organization can gain clarity around the nature of the leader's work practically and culturally to be successful in the role. This perspective can help the organization understand and prioritize what types of experience or leadership styles would thrive within the organization.

Communication and Transitioning of Key Relationships

A priority in organizations experiencing a leadership change is to be thoughtful about how and when to communicate that this change is taking place both internally and externally. A leadership change can be a cause of great uncertainty and potential turnover among internal staff. As a result, engaging the staff as a key thought partner in the process can pay huge dividends. Laying out the timeline for a planned leadership change and incorporating the perspectives of key staff members on what skills and traits the new leader should possess can help to gain buy-in and limit the possibility of a further drain of talent.

Likewise, having open conversations about the transition with key funders and strategic partners can help ensure your relationships with them are not damaged in the process. Allow your key stakeholders to learn the new voice and face before the leader is formally identified, ensuring that they can form a connection and that the transfer to your new leadership is seamless. What you want to avoid is a situation where the outgoing leader was the only person who communicated with a key constituency of your community. Identify the most critical donor/partner/stakeholder relationships and create a plan to involve more people from your organization in these relationships, ensuring that these vital connections stay intact after the leader departs.

Prior to my departure from Pitch In for Baseball and Softball, I made a conscious effort to include more staff members in planning calls with partners and major donors. In many cases, I relinquished my role as the primary contact so that my future exit wouldn't alter the nature of these vital relationships. That decision helped ensure a seamless transition to a new PIFBS contact with the ultimate result that the organization retained its key partnerships after I left.

Creating an Accurate Job Description

In many cases, the board may not have a clear sense of what the CEO's job is like on a day-to-day basis, or even how they do what they do. One way to bridge this knowledge gap is for the outgoing chief executive to make sure they commit as much of what they do in writing as possible. By systematizing and articulating the work you do on an ongoing basis, they will create a clearer sense of what is expected of the new leader and give them a shorter learning curve for when they eventually join the team.

The best perspective for this type of cataloging of your work would be to ask the question, "What information would you have appreciated when you first started, to help you understand what was expected of you and how to get it done?" This kind of a work audit can and should go from a broader perspective on how you spend your time to the nitty gritty of passwords, administrative logins, banking authority, and anything that would facilitate a smooth transition for the new leader.

The end result of this process could culminate in the outgoing executive creating a draft job description for the hiring committee. While the committee will ultimately decide what qualities and responsibilities it wants to include in the job description, having the perspective of the outgoing leader will create a more informed approach for the hiring process and clearer expectations for the eventual replacement.

The Role of the Outgoing Executive Director

In many situations, the outgoing Executive Director is retained for a limited period of time to help onboard the new leader and to counsel them as needed as they acclimate to their new role. In other situations, there is a conscious effort for the outgoing leader to not be present physically in the workplace, to help the new leader establish themselves without the shadow of the old guard being around. If the outgoing leader is a person who is leaving on good terms, it may be important for the board to consider what type of an off-ramp they would like to create for the outbound leader so that their final chapter with the organization is one that respects the role and impact they had on the success of the entity. In the end, the board will negotiate a plan with the outgoing executive that they feel best meets the needs of the new leader, the outgoing leader, and the staff as a whole. It's not an easy needle to thread, but it is one that can be accomplished with the right amount of attention and consideration.

An Exit Strategy Case Study

Gary Bagley has been in leadership roles in the nonprofit sector for over 25 years. He went through a thorough process when he decided to leave New York Cares after 13 years as their CEO. In his case, the exit wasn't driven by the usual reasons.

- He wasn't leaving for another job.
- He wasn't being fired.
- He wasn't retiring.

For him, the timing of the decision came down to two basic things: the organization's readiness to take on the hiring of a new leader and his readiness to leave the agency.

For the organization, Gary considered and assessed the following:

- **A stable and engaged Board**. Gary made an assessment that the board was more than capable of taking on the critical responsibility of hiring a new leader. "I was working with an experienced Board President and a highly engaged board. The exit of a leader and the search for their successor is arguably the time that a board is taking on its most important duty, so this was especially important to me."

- **Regular succession planning.** At New York Cares, one executive committee meeting per year was dedicated to succession planning (and had been for the last eight years or so of his tenure). This was not only about Gary and his role. It was about staff morale, advancement for staff, the pipeline for senior roles in the organization, and Board of Directors membership. All of this was critical information for navigating the impending period of transition.

- **A generally understood strategy.** According to Gary, "We were at a point where all stakeholders understood the direction the organization was going. It wasn't that everything was crystal clear (and there will always be unknown elements), but the general direction was clear and the conversations we needed to have were actively taking place. What a perfect time for a board to decide on a new leader."

In terms of his own personal readiness to leave and the process he undertook, Gary was equally methodical and introspective. He highlighted these key steps:

- **Get outside help.** "I preferred an executive coach, but you can also turn to your family, therapist, friends, or colleagues. You will likely consider many options, as did I. Having someone to help me throughout the process of examination (without falling into analysis paralysis), reminded me of what's important to me and cheered me on as I gained clarity."

- **Revisit your purpose**. Through the coaching process, Gary was reminded that purpose evolves, sometimes with age, sometimes with experience, and sometimes just because it does. He acknowledged that his purpose (being of service) had not changed, and that his job was just one way to be of service among many (paid and unpaid).

- **Decide what is next**. Gary developed an intentional plan and timeline for charting a new course. He stayed in touch with his executive coach during this time so that as new ideas began to bubble up, he had a sounding board for how to go about exploring them.

- **Pick an end date**. And finally, "Putting an end date on your tenure makes it real for you and everyone else. You can be flexible and provide a little support if the organization needs you for a bit longer, but the understanding that you are finished and leaving at a designated time is good for your board and your team."

Summary

Replacing an outgoing Executive Director is a watershed moment for an organization, one that can have a profound impact on both the current staff and the future success of the agency. While the hiring of the new leader is ultimately the responsibility of the Board of Directors, the outgoing executive can play an important role in helping the board understand which skills and personality traits might be critical for a new leader to be successful in their role. Succession planning doesn't have to be a topic that is too sensitive to talk about. Mature organizations recognize and anticipate the inevitability of leadership changes and plan accordingly.

Actionable Next Steps

1. Create a draft of the Executive Director job description if one doesn't exist.

2. If one does exist, review and amend it based on your recent experience.

3. Set up a meeting with your Board President to raise the general question of how the board/organization has prepared for the eventual change in leadership within your agency.

4. Encourage the board to create a committee that will meet periodically to create a hiring process that can be activated if and when a leadership change takes place.

CHAPTER 16:
Advice For New Leaders

Chapter Overview: In this chapter, the subject matter experts who contributed to this book offer advice to new leaders who might be entering an organization or this role for the first time.

During the course of writing this book I talked to almost two dozen nonprofit leaders and subject matter experts. While those conversations varied greatly based on their experience and perspective, one element of consistency was asking each of these individuals what advice they would give to someone who was new to the Executive Director role or was entering a new organization. What follows is a compilation of those nuggets of wisdom.

Go on Listening Tours

About half of the interviewees referenced the importance of some type of listening tour when joining a new organization. Taking the time to meet with every board member, key staff members, and your top funders within the first 60-90 days can be invaluable.

The structure of those conversations can vary but an approach that some leaders employ is to have a few simple structured questions:

1. What brought you to the organization in the first place?
2. What do you think we do particularly well?
3. What opportunities do you think we could pursue?

Over time hopefully patterns will develop. When they do, you will develop a clearer sense of the organization's capabilities and potential pathways to success. You may also spot some areas where the organization may need support in order to get back on track. People will appreciate the opportunity to share their point of view openly. You will begin the long and important process of building relationships with people throughout the organization.

Find or Build a Cohort of Other Leaders

Another common theme for speaking with leaders is the notion that being an Executive Director/CEO can be a lonely job. There is an understandable reluctance to be willing to open up to staff or board members. But as humans, especially leaders who may be under stress to help solve major organizational challenges, you need an outlet and people to talk to.

One solution is to be intentional and to seek out other leaders you can meet and talk to on a regular basis. Building this cohort could develop into a mechanism for you to open up and share challenges that you may be facing. Sometimes the simple act of knowing that others are facing similar hurdles can be therapeutic. In other situations, those peers may have helpful strategies you can employ to help navigate those choppy seas. Make these meetings, whether they be weekly coffees or monthly happy hours, priorities so that you cultivate a support network as you grow into this leadership role.

Be Patient

Things may just take longer than you may expect. While you may come into the organization with high expectations and a desire to make an immediate impact, it is also worth noting that not having a lay of the land can dramatically influence the timeline anticipated for whatever initiatives you are seeking to advance. Taking the time to get to know the people and processes that exist within the organization will pay dividends. You can't always go from step one to step 10 without taking all the steps along the way.

People Do Things for Different Reasons

While we might ideally believe that everyone has come to your organization with the same clear minded commitment to helping your organization achieve its mission, the reality is that people do things for different reasons. Whether they are staff, volunteers, or donors, it is important to create space for the idea that people do things for a variety of motivations. Don't judge that. Embrace it.

Be Consistent

Despite the instinct to come in early, make big promises, and try to make sweeping changes early, it is best to build an approach to work that is measured, consistent, and sustainable. People will look to how you do things and will likely notice if/when that approach changes. Consistency is an often overlooked quality among leaders.

Carve Out Resources for Self Care and Personal Growth

Within a very short period of time, a new leader will likely have an unending and insurmountable list of things to do for others and the organization. There may also be a dynamic of staff or budget scarcity. While it may feel selfish at first, it is important to develop an expectation that the organization should invest in your professional development. Building new skills, understanding how new technologies can impact your organization, and attending workshops and conferences take money and time to accomplish. Likewise, maintaining your exercise regimen, eating well, and not burning the midnight oil will also increase your ability to avoid burnout in this leadership role.

Speak Up

Although listening is the prevailing sentiment for new leaders, it is also ok to speak your mind after you have listened. Many new leaders may feel it's not their place to speak up. On the contrary, don't hold back. This doesn't mean you shouldn't be tactful and aware of how sharing certain "news" may be received, but it's highly unlikely you will be fired for speaking the truth. You were hired to be a leader and there is an expectation that you will provide your perspective on how the organization is doing and where it can improve.

Trust Yourself and Your Vision

Be driven by your own vision, and not everyone else's opinion. Everyone is going to have an opinion of your work and everybody wants to tell you how to do your job. Everybody thinks, without saying it, that they can do your job better than you can. People's input is very important. It is critical. I'm not saying it is not and it doesn't serve a purpose. But we can't base all our decisions as the top leader on everybody else's opinion. We gotta roll with our gut a lot. Everybody can't be an Executive Director. Being able to trust your instincts and make decisions is what makes you different. It's what makes you a leader.

Observe Your Programs

If you are new to the organization, get out there and see your programs in action. See how your staff and volunteers interact with your constituents. Try as much as possible to just stay in the shadows to watch and listen. If you can't sit back, ask open-ended questions like, "What do you like about this program?" or "How did you find out about us?"

Come in as a Curious Collaborator

While you may have some preconceived ideas about what needs to be done to help the organization succeed, come in as a curious learner. Ask questions of everyone. Get a range of perspectives.

Bring people together to discuss challenges the organization is facing. Facilitate, but don't lead these conversations.

Don't be Afraid to Tell People "I Don't Know"

Just because you are the new boss doesn't mean you have to have all the answers. The most surefire way for something to come back and bite you is to pretend you have the right answer when you don't. Being new gives you full permission to tell someone you will need to get back to them with the right answer.

Keep Asking Questions Until You Understand the Answer

Especially when it comes to financial statements, keep asking questions until you fully understand the situation. It's fair game to question the likelihood of certain gifts coming in. That is not a reflection on your development team. It's ok to ask about prior program expenses. That doesn't mean your program staff are being wasteful. Question everything.

Ask Donors for Their Opinion, Not for Money

As the new leader, just because you may be the primary fundraiser doesn't mean you should ask prior big funders for money the first time you meet them. Ask them a lot of questions.

- How is the organization doing?
- Why do you support us?
- What do you think we do particularly well?
- What do you think we can do better?

Taking this approach will not only build your knowledge of your key funders, but will build their relationship with you as well. They will like that you asked them their opinion.

Focus on the "Why"

In conversations with everyone you come into contact with for the first time, be a sponge – especially on their motivations. Probe their "why." Don't assume you know what drives people. Ask them.

- Why do you like working here?
- Why do you volunteer your time here?
- Why do you donate to us?
- Why does your company like to associate with us?

Find Out What Fills Your Tank

This job might be hard, especially in the beginning. Find out what activities seem to drain you of energy and find a way to outsource or delegate them. Find out what activities fill you with energy and schedule more of them into your calendar. If observing certain aspects of your program fills you up, then do it regularly. If something else drains your passion and energy, find a way to reduce your exposure to it.

Actionable Next Steps

Scan this QR code to stay in touch. Connect with me on LinkedIn and let me know more about you and your journey as a nonprofit leader. I will also add you to my email distribution list so you can be the first to know about new content and other events related to nonprofit leadership.

CONTRIBUTOR PROFILES

Elizabeth Abel

Background:

- Partners with nonprofit institutions to plan and implement multi-million-to-billion dollar campaigns

- Senior Vice President at CCS Fundraising, a global fundraising consulting firm for nonprofits and an instructor at the University of Pennsylvania

- Recognized for her philanthropic leadership by the New York Jewish Week in their 2024 "36 to Watch" and by BELLA Magazine as a "Woman of Influence in Philanthropy"

Where in the book?

Chapter 3: Building Your Fundraising Strategy

Individual Giving

Why were you interested in contributing to "Passion Isn't Enough"?

It is a privilege to contribute to this project and to support nonprofit professionals as they lead important mission-driven work.

How do you think "Passion Isn't Enough" will be valuable to nonprofit leaders?

"Passion Isn't Enough" will be a valuable resource for nonprofit leaders, whether they are seasoned professionals seeking to enhance their skills or just beginning their career in the nonprofit sector.

Scan this QR code to connect with Elizabeth on LinkedIn:

Gary Bagley

Background:

- Over 25 years experience in the nonprofit sector, most recently as Executive Director of New York Cares, NYC's largest organization devoted to driving community impact through volunteer-led programs

- Previous experiences include positions at nonprofit organizations focused on arts education - Young Audiences New York and TADA! Youth Theater

- Teaches nonprofit leadership, management, and strategy at Columbia University and Baruch College

Where in the book?

Chapter 15: Building Your Exit Strategy

An Exit Strategy Case Study

Why were you interested in contributing to "Passion Isn't Enough"?

I especially appreciated that David wanted to share case studies in addition to theoretical perspectives. I'm happy to share my personal experience if it is helpful to other leaders grappling with the same issue.

How do you think "Passion Isn't Enough" will be valuable to nonprofit leaders?

The life of a nonprofit leader is a constant juggling act. Books that teach us or remind us of the standards we can uphold and ways we can go about our work in a smart way are a lifesaver.

Scan this QR code to connect with Gary on his website:

Doug Bauer

Background:

- Works with an array of nonprofit organizations and their leaders across the globe on a variety of issues

- Is part of the management team and launched a philanthropic Advisor firm (Rockefeller Philanthropy Advisors)

- Teaches courses on philanthropy and the nonprofit sector at Columbia and Penn

Where in the book?

Chapter 7: Building Your Evidence Base

The Importance of Measurement and Evaluation

Why were you interested in contributing to "Passion Isn't Enough"?

I have great respect for David and his perspective on the work of nonprofits. He is one of the few business leaders who has made a successful transition to the nonprofit sector but has not forgotten the skills he honed in the private sector.

How do you think "Passion Isn't Enough" will be valuable to nonprofit leaders?

In general, nonprofit management books have been uneven in terms of content and the quality of that content. David is a pragmatist (with a sense of humor) and brings a thoughtful perspective to the advice and counsel he shares with nonprofit managers and executives and the board members that support them. I expect the book to be an extension of David's take on what works and what does not in the third sector.

Scan this QR code to connect with Doug on LinkedIn:

Rich Berlin

Background:

- Founding Chair of DREAM Charter School, served as DREAM's Executive Director since 1997 and became co-Chief Executive Officer alongside Eve Colavito in 2021

- Began his journey with DREAM as a volunteer baseball coach in 1994. During his tenure, DREAM has grown from a summer recreation program with one staff member to a thriving community-based organization recognized locally and nationally with numerous awards for programmatic and operational excellence

- DREAM now serves over 2,000 youth from pre-K to pre-college across East Harlem and the South Bronx through a growing network of inclusive, extended-day, extended-year charter schools and community sports-based youth development programs

Where in the book?

Chapter 8: Building Your Brand

The 4Ps and the 7Ps -> Proof

Chapter 11: Building Your Team

Hiring; Onboarding

Why were you interested in contributing to "Passion Isn't Enough"?

Not only do I have great respect for David as a leader in the sector, I am honored to be a part of any project that advances best practices in leadership or supports leaders more generally in this very hard work.

How do you think "Passion Isn't Enough" will be valuable to nonprofit leaders?

Nonprofit leadership is very hard, lonely work. Anything that connects leadership in a shared understanding of the difficult task and offers some hints of recognition or even inspiration is worth the read.

Scan this QR code to connect with Rich on LinkedIn:

Jeffrey Breslin

Background:

- Created Project Rampart - Under Armour's comprehensive investment in Baltimore City public school athletics

- Led the creation of the Baltimore Ravens Boys & Girls Club and UA House at Fayette - two signature youth development facilities

- Supported hundreds of communities through youth development programs at Cal Ripken, Sr. Foundation

Where in the book?

Chapter 6: Building Your Programs

Managing Change

Why were you interested in contributing to "Passion Isn't Enough"?

My own experience leading a growing nonprofit organization while attempting to navigate the many challenges that come with the job made me appreciate a great resource like David's book.

How do you think "Passion Isn't Enough" will be valuable to nonprofit leaders?

Learning from the experience of others is a key trait of a successful leader, especially when doing it for the first time!

Scan this QR code to connect with Jeffrey on LinkedIn:

Beth S. Brodovsky

Background:

- Spent over 35 years committed to helping nonprofits build and manage their brands

- Hosted the 200-episode "Driving Participation" podcast

- Provided workshops and trainings that have grown the skills of thousands of nonprofit marketers

Where in the book?

Chapter 9: Building Your Communications Strategy

Target Audience; Lovers, Likers, and Haters; The Customer Journey

Why were you interested in contributing to "Passion Isn't Enough"?

In general - David has been such a supporter of my work and ideas, and I am thrilled to participate in anything he requests of me.

Specifically - The idea of branding and marketing for a nonprofit is not always valued in the sector. I want nonprofits to understand how strategic thinking in these areas will create a path for delivering on their strategic plan. It all starts with audience focus.

How do you think "Passion Isn't Enough" will be valuable to nonprofit leaders?

Having the skills to deliver on your goals allows passion to thrive. When you know how to achieve what you want to achieve, you can keep that spark alive.

Scan this QR code to connect with Beth on her website:

Julia Campbell

Background:

- Named as a top thought leader and one to follow by Forbes and LinkedIn for Nonprofits, and one of the 30 Nonprofit IT Influencers to Follow in 2024

- Her books: "Storytelling in the Digital Age: A Guide for Nonprofits" and "How to Build and Mobilize a Social Media Community for Your Nonprofit"

- Launched Social Media for Social Good Academy, the first online training course for Nonprofit social media managers. Also founded and organizes the annual Nonprofit Social Media Summit, a live event for nonprofits and hosts the weekly podcast Nonprofit Nation

Where in the book?

Chapter 9: Building Your Communications Strategy

Communications Vehicles -> Social Media

Why were you interested in contributing to "Passion Isn't Enough"?

I appreciate and respect David Rhode, and I enjoy talking about how nonprofits can best leverage social media.

How do you think "Passion Isn't Enough" will be valuable to nonprofit leaders?

Passion IS NOT enough. Nonprofit leaders need tactics, techniques, and actionable insights in order to translate their passion into a sustainable organization.

Scan this QR code to connect with Julia on LinkedIn:

Jackie Einstein Astrof

Background:

- Founder of PennPAC, a national pro bono consulting program that assists nonprofit organizations with their strategic business challenges, oftentimes providing transformational change

- After 13 years, PennPAC has assisted 250 nonprofits across three cities (and beyond) engaging nearly 2,000 volunteers to donate 50,000 direct service hours valued at over $10M

Where in the book?

Chapter 6: Building Your Programs

Program Growth

Chapter 13: Building Your Volunteer Community

Leaning into Volunteer Engagement

Why were you interested in contributing to "Passion Isn't Enough"?

David has so much practical advice and experience and is a great articulator. This book will be a great resource to nonprofit leaders.

How do you think "Passion Isn't Enough" will be valuable to nonprofit leaders?

See above!

Scan this QR code to connect with Jackie on LinkedIn:

Cynthia Figueroa

Background:

- Served as Deputy Mayor for the City of Philadelphia. During COVID, created access centers for children who did not have access to internet so that they would not fall behind during the school year

- Developed food sites for children and families during COVID

- Served in two Mayoral Administrations and was CEO for three nonprofits

Where in the book?

Chapter 6: Building Your Programs

Assessing Existing Programs; Understanding Program Costs

Why were you interested in contributing to "Passion Isn't Enough"?

To support and improve nonprofit operations, and future success and sustainability of future nonprofits.

How do you think "Passion Isn't Enough" will be valuable to nonprofit leaders?

I believe that insight based on real life experiences will be of value to future and current nonprofits. The many experiences of nonprofit leaders in the nonprofit sector is important to help guide the future leaders in the nonprofit world.

Scan this QR code to connect with Cynthia on LinkedIn:

Greg Goldman

Background:

- Senior Program Officer, The Philadelphia Foundation; Executive Director, MANNA, Wireless Philadelphia, and Audubon PA

- Executive search professional with DiverseForce, focusing on placing c-suite leaders in social impact organizations

- Nearly 30 years on faculty at UPenn in the Urban Studies Program and the Nonprofit Leadership Program at the School of Social Policy and Practice

Where in the book?

Chapter 12: Building Your Diverse Organization

Bringing a Diversity Lens to Your Organization

Why were you interested in contributing to "Passion Isn't Enough"?

David Rhode is a creative and thoughtful nonprofit leader whose varied career in business and as a social entrepreneur makes his insights into the sector uniquely valuable. I am thrilled that he was willing to devote his time to gathering and sharing the best practices that he has learned and deployed in his career.

How do you think "Passion Isn't Enough" will be valuable to nonprofit leaders?

Having the opportunity to hear directly from similarly situated leaders--what were their successes and what were their challenges--is extremely helpful to social impact Executive Directors and CEOs. These jobs can be lonely and the dilemmas can be hard to solve. A book like this is like having a mentor or a peer group to help you hone your leadership skills, feel confident in your decision-making, and bounce back stronger from any setbacks you encounter.

Scan this QR code to connect with Greg on LinkedIn:

David C. Harris

Background:

- Managing Partner of Interim Executive Solutions

- Co-Chair of Community Action Partners (Pro-bono Consulting)

- Interim ED for several nonprofits

Where in the book?

Chapter 15: Building Your Exit Strategy

Key Decisions in a Hiring Process -> Considering Interim Leadership

Why were you interested in contributing to "Passion Isn't Enough"?

As interim leaders entering organizations that frequently have many diagnosed and undiagnosed challenges, we have learned a lot about the leadership skills needed to bring the team together and create a solid foundation for future success.

How do you think "Passion Isn't Enough" will be valuable to nonprofit leaders?

Successful, sustainable nonprofits do not depend on one individual or even a shared commitment to a vision. Rather, responsibility, accountability and commitment to the mission must be infused throughout the organization so it can continue to function and thrive in the face of inevitable change.

Scan this QR code to connect with David on his website:

Eileen R. Heisman

Background:

- President and CEO of National Philanthropic Trust from 1998-2024; built NPT into the premier "white glove" provider of DAFs; raised $50 billion and services more than 17k client DAF accounts

- Co-convened a group of national industry leaders who regularly educate federal and state policymakers regarding DAF industry best practices relative to proposed regulation

- Has overseen NPT's annual Donor-Advised Fund Report

Where in the book?

Chapter 3: Building Your Fundraising Strategy

The Fundraising Landscape

Why were you interested in contributing to "Passion Isn't Enough"?

As a long-time instructor at the University of Pennsylvania, I support the learning of philanthropy and all aspects of the nonprofit sector. I have a personal interest in mentorship and "paying it forward." Contributing to a project such as this reinforces that mission for me.

How do you think "Passion Isn't Enough" will be valuable to nonprofit leaders?

No matter where you are in your career as a nonprofit leader, there are always new ideas and ways to approach the work differently. Often nonprofit leaders will come to the work with a concentration of knowledge in one part of the sector, but not all parts. I hope that this book will help strengthen areas of expertise for all readers.

Scan this QR code to connect with Eileen on LinkedIn:

Kenny Holdsman

Background:

- Served as Philly Youth Basketball's President and CEO, as well as co-founder since 2015; oversees all organizational aspects including strategic planning, fund development, board development and engagement, and community partnerships

- Served as President of Legacy Youth Tennis and Education (formerly Arthur Ashe) from February 2009-June 2015, created the W.K. Kellogg Youth Innovation Fund, and staffed the Campaign for Civic Mission of Schools

- Served as the Director of Service-Learning and Youth Leadership in the School District of Philadelphia and the Co-Director of Philadelphia Freedom Schools

Where in the book?

Chapter 3: Building Your Fundraising Strategy

Capital Campaigns

Why were you interested in contributing to "Passion Isn't Enough"?

I hold David Rhode in high regard as a nonprofit leader and thinker.

How do you think "Passion Isn't Enough" will be valuable to nonprofit leaders?

A book like "Passion Isn't Enough" will be valuable to nonprofit leaders to fuel continuous improvement and reflection by hearing the stories of other nonprofit leaders.

Scan this QR code to connect with Kenny through Philadelphia Youth Basketball:

Remy Reya

Background:

- Led a national organization (Compass Pro Bono) through multiple major operational transitions—including a headquarters office relocation, an internal tech overhaul, and a staff function reshuffling—while maintaining seamless collaboration and impact delivery

- Project-managed and codified processes for execution of key fundraising and thought leadership initiatives at Compass Pro Bono, including their end-of-year fundraising campaign and annual board training conference

- Led Compass Pro Bono volunteer consultant teams to conduct deep research and deliver more than $400k worth of pro bono strategic consulting to two DC-area nonprofits: Arlington Thrive in clarifying their organizational value proposition, and Pathways to Housing DC to better support frontline staff

Where in the book?

Chapter 13: Building Your Volunteer Community

Leaning into Volunteer Engagement

Why were you interested in contributing to "Passion Isn't Enough"?

Compass Pro Bono has curated strategic engagements to support local nonprofits for over 20 years; only in the last few have we begun to translate this institutional knowledge into shareable lessons for other organizations. At every turn, we've found that peeling back the curtain on what we've learned has paid dividends—both by helping other mission-driven organizations supercharge their work and strengthening ties within the nonprofit communities we're in.

How do you think "Passion Isn't Enough" will be valuable to nonprofit leaders?

The value of knowledge- and resource-sharing in the nonprofit sector can't be overstated. Books like this one are essential opportunities to clarify the path to greater impact for emerging social impact leaders.

Scan this QR code to connect with Remy on LinkedIn:

Dr. Jocelynne Rainey

Background:

- Over 30 years of nonprofit management experience

- Architect of a best-in-class workforce development program at the Brooklyn Navy Yard

- CEO of BKO where under her leadership they rebranded and have become a model of community-led philanthropy where everyone can engage

Where in the book?

Chapter 8: Building Your Brand

Rebranding

Why were you interested in contributing to "Passion Isn't Enough"?

Nonprofits are often the heart of a community. They bring resources and stability to those that need it that often result in outcomes for individuals, families, and communities that improve not only their lives but the lives of all. So many outstanding people have benefited from these services and the leadership of these organizations are critical to this success. I am hopeful that sharing my experience will help other leaders as I have been helped in the past.

How do you think "Passion Isn't Enough" will be valuable to nonprofit leaders?

The work of nonprofits is so important and complex to all communities and the leaders must be passionate. However, in order for nonprofits to thrive and scale as needed, leaders must also be equipped with the tools and knowledge they need to support and protect the nonprofit "business." "Passion Isn't Enough" will be that tool.

Scan this QR code to connect with Jocelynne through Brooklyn Org:

Brooke Richie-Babbage

Background:

- Founder and CEO of Bending Arc, a social impact strategy firm partnering with social change leaders and philanthropic institutions around the country

- Founded/led multiple successful organizations/initiatives, such as: the Resilience Advocacy Project (RAP), the Sterling Network NYC, the NetLab Initiative, both initiatives at the Robert Sterling Clark Foundation, and the Urban Justice Center's Social Justice Accelerator initiative

- Served as visiting lecturer and featured speaker at numerous top law schools and presented papers throughout the U.S. on social entrepreneurship, non-profit leadership, and community lawyering

Where in the book?

Chapter 1: Building Your Strategic Plan

How Far Ahead Should My Strategic Plan Look?

Chapter 11: Building Your Team

Hiring

Why were you interested in contributing to "Passion Isn't Enough"?

I was excited to participate in this project because I'm deeply passionate about building the capacity of institutions doing social impact work, and because I believe that David's book will make an important contribution to our sector.

How do you think "Passion Isn't Enough" will be valuable to nonprofit leaders?

Well-run, high-impact nonprofits make our society stronger and better. Yet so much of what it takes to make a nonprofit effective can feel messy, opaque, and even overwhelming to even the most passionate and committed nonprofit professional. David's concrete and practical articulation of critical nonprofit principles cuts through the messiness. The book can serve as a playbook for people in our sector who want to do their work better, and make their organizations stronger.

Scan this QR code to connect with Brooke through her website:

Scott Rosenkrans

Background:

- Entire career has been spent in the nonprofit sector

- Has built predictive models for 10+ years; overseen AI predictive models for 6+ years

- Recognized by Fast Company magazine in their 2020 World Changing Ideas issue

Where in the book?

Chapter 10: Building Your AI Capabilities

Introduction; Where to Start with AI

Why were you interested in contributing to "Passion Isn't Enough"?

I was eager to participate in this project because I believe in the transformative power of knowledge sharing, especially in the nonprofit sector. Having spent over a decade working at the intersection of AI and nonprofit fundraising, I understand the unique challenges and opportunities that nonprofit leaders face. Contributing to a resource that aims to equip these leaders with practical tools and insights aligns perfectly with my mission to advance the sector through innovative and responsible use of technology.

How do you think "Passion Isn't Enough" will be valuable to nonprofit leaders?

"Passion Isn't Enough" is a crucial resource for nonprofit leaders because it bridges the gap between enthusiasm and effective leadership. While passion is a powerful motivator, it must be complemented by strategic thinking, practical skills, and a deep understanding of the evolving landscape of nonprofit work. This book, enriched by the diverse experiences and expertise of over 20 leaders, provides actionable guidance that can help nonprofit executives navigate their roles more effectively and sustainably, ensuring their organizations thrive in the long term.

Scan this QR code to connect with Scott on LinkedIn:

LaVonté A. Stewart

Background:

- Founding Executive Director, Lost Boyz Inc.

- Grown organization's operating revenue as high as $1.9 Million

- Became a leading voice in the area of Sports Based Youth Development

Where in the book?

Chapter 11: Building Your Team

Hiring

Why were you interested in contributing to "Passion Isn't Enough"?

David is an amazing person and wonderful professional. David and Pitch In for Baseball and Softball directly contributed to the rapid growth of our organization and my personal development in the field.

How do you think "Passion Isn't Enough" will be valuable to nonprofit leaders?

The book will share insights with a very unique perspective only someone steeped in sports could give.

Scan this QR code to connect with LaVonté on LinkedIn:

Sharmila Rao Thakkar

Background:

- Executive Director of P-Squared Philanthropies; partners with foundation principles to guide the foundation's direction and activities in service to its mission

- Adjunct Associate Faculty and Instructor of Nonprofit Management at Columbia University's School of Professional Studies

- Advises and coaches donors, families, and organizations on operations, strategy, governance, multigenerational engagement, equity and inclusion, grantmaking, and community outreach

Where in the book?

Chapter 2: Building Your Board

Board Governance

Why were you interested in contributing to "Passion Isn't Enough"?

I highly respect David and his work. So when he reached out to describe the book he was working on, I was honored to participate! It was such a treat to be in conversation with

David about the importance of governance and board development to understanding and building an effective model for nonprofit leadership.

How do you think "Passion Isn't Enough" will be valuable to nonprofit leaders?

In my coaching of EDs and training/onboarding for prospective and current board members, "passion is not enough" is a resounding theme throughout. This book will be invaluable to nonprofit leaders because it will provide insight on the importance of combining enthusiasm and dedication with strategic thinking, practical skills and continued learning. It promises to be a go-to guide for nonprofit leaders aiming to adopt structured approaches to governance, leadership, and organizational development, essential for creating sustainable impact and fulfilling a nonprofit's mission.

Scan this QR code to connect with Sharmila on LinkedIn:

Farra Trompeter

Background:

- Have developed branding, communications, and fundraising strategies and campaigns for nonprofits for 30 years; Host of The Smart Communications Podcast

- Have been an adjunct professor for graduate students studying nonprofit management at New York University, CUNY Baruch College, and The New School

- Have served on several nonprofit boards, including NTEN and the NYC Anti-Violence Project

Where in the book?

Chapter 8: Building Your Brand

What is a Brand?; Rebranding

Why were you interested in contributing to "Passion Isn't Enough"?

Branding and communications often happen in ad hoc and reactive ways in nonprofits. In all of my work, I strive to provide insights that help leaders understand how to leverage the power of communications.

How do you think "Passion Isn't Enough" will be valuable to nonprofit leaders?

Nonprofit leaders are often juggling multiple and competing demands for their attention. They rarely have enough time, finances, or human resources to do all that is required of them. A book with practical advice and tips can help nonprofit leaders sharpen their skills which will ultimately influence how well they can support their team in achieving the organization's mission.

Scan this QR code to connect with Farra on LinkedIn:

Liz Wainger

Background:

- Seasoned communications consultant and strategist advising foundations and nonprofits on increasing their impact and influence

- Used experience working inside two large nonprofits and over 25 years as a consultant to help hundreds of organizations illuminate value, build revenue and reputations, and break down internal silos

- Worked with a wide array of organizations from health care, to affordable housing, community finance, and arts and culture, helping them find the right messages and strategies to attract and retain staff and donors and craft messaging that engages target audiences to support the delivery of their vital missions

Where in the book?

Chapter 14: Building Your Crisis Response

Building Your Crisis Response Plan; Striking the Right Tone in Your Communications

Why were you interested in contributing to "Passion Isn't Enough"?

Throughout my 25-year career, I have seen too many nonprofits unable to fully fulfill their promise because they have not been able to tell their story effectively or have made missteps that cause them to lose key audiences so critical to their success. Nonprofits lack the time and resources to invest properly in themselves. This project provides nonprofit leaders and their teams with those very resources that are so needed and I am happy to lend my expertise to this larger mission.

How do you think "Passion Isn't Enough" will be valuable to nonprofit leaders?

Nonprofits lack the time and resources to invest properly in themselves. "Passion Isn't Enough" provides nonprofit leaders and their teams with the expertise and resources at their fingertips that they desperately need.

Scan this QR code to connect with Liz through her website:

Joe Waters

Background:

- Twenty years of experience working in the nonprofit sector on win-win partnerships

- Writes the leading blog on cause marketing and corporate partnerships on the web

- Has written two books on win-win partnerships: Cause Marketing for Dummies and Fundraising with Businesses

Where in the book?

Chapter 4: Building Your Partnership Portfolio

Meet Joe Waters

Why were you interested in contributing to "Passion Isn't Enough"?

If David asks you to be involved in something, you say yes! It has to be good!

How do you think "Passion Isn't Enough" will be valuable to nonprofit leaders?

"Passion Isn't Enough" will be valuable to nonprofit leaders because it emphasizes the importance of strategic planning, sustainable practices, and effective leadership beyond just passion.

The book offers practical tools and insights for navigating the challenges in the nonprofit sector, helping leaders build better and more impactful organizations.

Scan this QR code to connect with Joe through his website:

Colin A. Weil

Background:

- As Executive Director of Congregation B'nai Jeshurun, led one of America's oldest and most storied synagogue communities through a dynamic period of growth and change, including pivoting from in-person only to full multi-camera broadcast capabilities during COVID, and substantial restoration of a 100- year-old historic campus

- As Director of Marketing and Digital at The Jewish Museum, re-branded the storied 5th Avenue museum for the 21st Century, and built-out technology infrastructure including CRM, web, and social media

Where in the book?

Chapter 15: Building Your Exit Strategy

Preparing for a New Leader

Why were you interested in contributing to "Passion Isn't Enough"?

I believe deeply in the nonprofit sector, while also recognizing that it can perform better. I think David has excellent perspective on this and so was happy to collaborate.

How do you think "Passion Isn't Enough" will be valuable to nonprofit leaders?

As a nonprofit professional and/or lay leader of multiple institutions over more than three decades, I have experienced the incredible opportunities offered when personal passion meets mission, but also the challenges created when passion gets in the way of good strategy. I believe David's book will help nonprofit leaders see the landscape fully, and thereby accentuate the opportunities while minimizing the risks.

Scan this QR code to connect with Colin on LinkedIn:

ACKNOWLEDGMENTS

Embarking on a first book project is both an act of faith and a testament to the old cliche "it takes a village." At the outset, I want to thank my wife, Helaine, for her encouragement to write this book. Her support and willingness to allow me to try to find a quiet space to write in a New York City apartment has been invaluable. I also want to thank my children, Tyler, Casey and Rebecca for their optimism and inspiration. Lastly, it wouldn't be a family shout out without recognizing my most faithful companion, Nala, who has sat at my feet for the vast majority of this project.

One of my first and best decisions in writing this book was partnering with Sierra Melcher and her team at Red Falcon Press. Sierra helped me see progress when I felt stuck and gave me the confidence to keep pushing ahead.

I also want to thank my lifelong friend, Carla Scholz, for providing her insight in the cover design process. While I ultimately didn't have the courage to embrace Carla's most bold thoughts,

I can't thank her enough for helping to bring consensus and sanity to the final stages of this piece of the puzzle.

A special thank you to Corrie Wiedmann and Celeste Flick, for not only being reliable running friends, but for taking the time to carefully proofread the manuscript.

Lastly, I want to recognize SJ Kounoupis for being my wingman over the last several months of the project. SJ was a student of mine at Penn and when I asked him to get involved to help with research and other vital tasks he jumped in with both feet. His editing talents, cheerleading, and attention to detail were essential to the final work product. SJ has a bright future and I am so glad we got to work closely together to make this book a reality. Thank you from the bottom of my heart feels inadequate, but for now it will have to suffice.

ABOUT THE AUTHOR

In 2005, David Rhode founded, led and scaled Pitch In For Baseball and Softball, a nonprofit organization that increased access to baseball and softball for children in under-resourced communities through the donation of equipment and uniforms.

After leaving Pitch In For Baseball and Softball in 2019, David founded Dot Dot Org, a nonprofit consulting firm focusing on CEO mentoring. David now teaches Nonprofit Branding and Nonprofit Consulting at the University of Pennsylvania. He is also the Deputy Director at PennPAC, an organization that mobilizes pro bono teams of University of Pennsylvania alumni as consultants to strengthen the nonprofit sector.

David studied undergraduate business and graduated Magna Cum Laude from Georgetown University. He graduated with Honors with an MBA from The Wharton School.

He is married with three children and is an avid Philadelphia sports fan. He and his family now live in New York City.

THANK YOU!

Thank you so much for reading "Passion Isn't Enough." This book was intended to be practical for those in nonprofit leadership positions. If you found it helpful, please share your review on Amazon so that other readers will have the confidence to add this resource to their toolkit.

Until we meet again,

David Rhode

www.ingramcontent.com/pod-product-compliance
Lightning Source LLC
Chambersburg PA
CBHW020533030426
42337CB00013B/832